D1603672

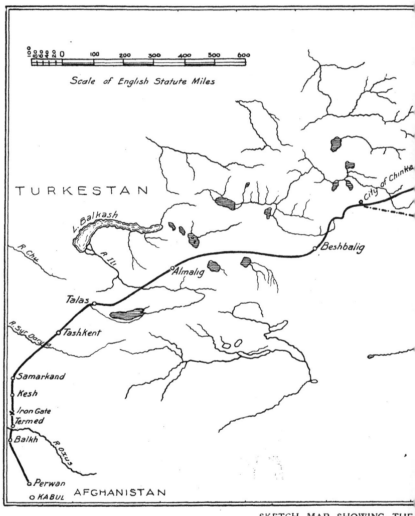

Scale of English Statute Miles

100 80 60 40 20 0   100   200   300   400   500   600

TURKESTAN

L. Balkash

R. Chu

R. Ili

R. Syr-Darya

Almalig

Talas

Tashkent

Samarkand

Kesh

Iron Gate

Termed

Balkh

R. Oxus

Perwan

KABUL

AFGHANISTAN

Beshbalig

City of Chinka

SKETCH MAP SHOWING THE
The dotted line shows the

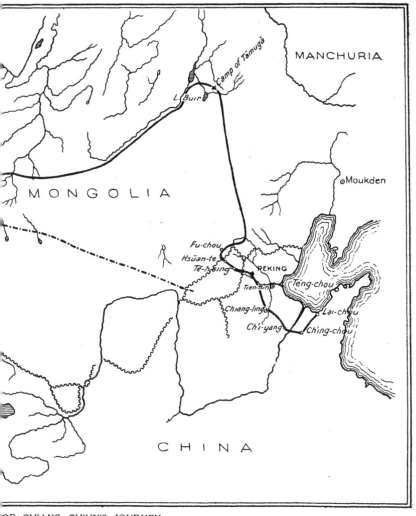

MANCHURIA

Camp of Tamuga

L. Buir

MONGOLIA

⊙Moukden

Fu-chou
Hsüan-te
Tê-hsing
PEKING
Tien-tsin
Têng-chou
Chiang-ling
Chi-yang
Lai-chou
Ching-chou

CHINA

OF CH'ANG CH'UN'S JOURNEY
of his route on his return

THE BROADWAY TRAVELLERS

EDITED BY SIR E. DENISON ROSS
AND EILEEN POWER

❧

THE TRAVELS OF
AN ALCHEMIST

THE JOURNEY OF THE TAOIST CH'ANG-CH'UN FROM CHINA TO THE HINDUKUSH AT THE SUMMONS OF CHINGIZ KHAN

Recorded by His Disciple
LI CHIH-CH'ANG

Translated with an Introduction by
ARTHUR WALEY

Published by
GEORGE ROUTLEDGE & SONS, LTD.
BROADWAY HOUSE, CARTER LANE, LONDON

First published in 1931

PRINTED IN GREAT BRITAIN BY HEADLEY BROTHERS,
LONDON AND ASHFORD, KENT.

LIST OF CONTENTS

v

PREFACE

THE editors of this series originally intended to publish an English translation of the Russian version of the *Hsi Yu Chi* made by the Archimandrite Palladius (born 1817; died 1878). But this version appeared over half a century ago, and in the meantime the progress in Chinese studies has been so great that the work of Palladius, admirable considering the date at which it was made, now requires considerable revision. In particular, his annotation is not merely out of date but was designed for a class of reader quite different from that to which the present series is addressed.

When, therefore, I was asked to revise the English translation I soon saw that not only a completely new annotation but also a fresh and independent translation from the Chinese text were indispensable if the book was to fit in with the general aims of the series. As regards Mongol history and philology, I have made constant use of M. Pelliot's researches. But in dealing with the history of medieval Taoism

PREFACE

I have ventured upon completely new ground, the subject having been scarcely touched upon either by European or by modern Chinese writers. The reason for this neglect has been the inaccessibility of the Taoist Canon. But since its re-publication by the Commercial Press of Shanghai in 1923-1925 this huge *corpus*, consisting of some fifteen hundred works, has been at the disposition of European scholars, and it is strange that they should hitherto have made so little use of it.

The *Hsi Yu Chi*, though its main interest is cultural and geographical, is also unique in its importance as a source for early Mongol history, enabling us as it does to fix with absolute certainty the otherwise obscure and much disputed dates of Chingiz Khan's movements during his Western campaign.

Following the general tendency of Chinese literature, the *Hsi Yu Chi* is in the highest degree impersonal. We do not get so much as a glimpse of the narrator's own character, nor of his personal relations with the rest of the mission. The physical sufferings of the travellers, their struggles against cold and heat, hunger and fatigue are alluded to in a general way. But the minor difficulties and vexations of the expedition, in which the individualities of the persons concerned would be most likely to be displayed, are passed over in complete silence. The problem of

PREFACE

language, for example, must have been an acute one. It is most improbable that Chin*k*ai, the Christian-Mongol leader of the expedition during its most trying phases, spoke any Chinese. Yet just as, by a poetic convention, Greek and Trojan heroes gird at one another in the same language, so Chin*k*ai speaks freely with the Chinese who were under his protection. How different, in its realism, is the narrative of William of Rubruck, who describes his gradual realization of the fact that when he said one thing his interpreter " totum aliud dicebat secundum quod ei occurrebat ".

For the general reader the chief appeal of the book lies in its successive pictures of widely-varying customs and races. Leaving the crowded Chinese plains, we see the Mongol nomads with their waggons and flocks, their fur-trimmed coats and strange head-dresses then the turbaned Moslem ploughman, the cosmopolitan crowds of Samarkand and the wild tribesmen of Afghanistan.

A feature of the narrative to which my translation does not do justice is the long series of poems by Ch'ang-ch'un which the narrator has inserted in his text. Most of these I have omitted. In the original they are no more than tolerably executed *vers d'occasion*. In translation it appears to me that they lose all point whatever, and the effort to torture them into a semblance of poetry would be a painful task. Ch'ang-ch'un has no reputation as a poet, and judging from the specimens in the *Hsi Yu Chi*, he deserves none. The reader may therefore feel assured that by the omission of the poems he is losing nothing of importance.

Two works have tended to be confused with the present *Hsi Yu Chi* :

(1) The *Hsi Yü Chi*, describing the pilgrimage to India of the great Buddhist traveller Hsüan-tsang (seventh century).

(2) The *Hsi Yu Chi* of Wu Ch'êng-ên (end of the sixteenth century), a fantastic novel which is to some extent a parody of the *Hsi Yü Chi* of Hsüan-tsang. For a long time it was supposed to be the work of Ch'ang-ch'un, a mistake only possible because till the nineteenth century very little was known either about Ch'ang-ch'un himself or about the book in which his travels are described.

Three further points require mention :

(1) The map, adapted from one in Bretschneider's *Medieval Researches*, is intended merely to give the reader a general idea of the course followed by Ch'ang-ch'un on his journey. To make a new and complete map was a task beyond the powers of the present editors and translator.

PREFACE

(2) The sounds which phoneticians write χ and γ are here transcribed k and g. For these sounds M. Pelliot writes q and γ; M. Grousset ḳ and ġ. An alternative would be kh and gh.

(3) Many philological points, such as Ch'ang-ch'un's Mongol title (p. 101), could not here be dealt with, owing to the impossibility of using Chinese characters.

INTRODUCTION

CHINA AND CENTRAL ASIA
AT THE TIME OF CH'ANG-CH'UN'S JOURNEY

AT the time of the Mongol invasions China was split up into three kingdoms: (1) the Sung empire, south of the Yangtze, the only one of the three that was native Chinese; (2) the Tangut kingdom, established in Kansu by a Tibeto-Burman people; (3) the kingdom of the Kin Tartars in Northern China; it was their territory that Europeans knew as Cathay. This name, however, does not properly belong to the Kins, but to their predecessors, the *K*itai. As this latter, an Eastern Mongol tribe, is frequently mentioned in this book and played an important part in Central Asian history, it will be convenient to give some account of its rise and migration.

The Kitai (Cathayans)

Taking advantage of the confusion that followed the fall of the T'ang dynasty at the end of the ninth century, these people began to press southward into China. In 938 they made their capital at Peking. The *K*itai rapidly absorbed Chinese culture, and in the thirteenth century a member of their ruling family, Yeh-lü Ch'u-ts'ai (often mentioned in the course of this book) became the moſt celebrated writer of his time. For more than 180 years the *K*itai reigned at Peking; but in 1114 they were attacked by a North Manchurian tribe, the Kin Tartars, who eventually captured Peking in 1123.

A certain number of *K*itai refused to submit to the Kins. We know that a band of fugitives, fleeing across the Mongolian desert, was crushed by the Lion *K*han, prince of Kashgar, in 1128 or a little later. Another sortie was deſtined to have much more important consequences. Yeh-lü Ta-shih, a member of the *K*itai royal family, managed to escape with a few hundred followers to seek protection from the Uighur prince of Beshbali*g*. Here Ta-shih collected an army and embarked upon a career of conqueſt as surprising in its way as that of Chingiz himself. In some half dozen years[1] (he died in 1135 or 1136) he built up an Empire that extended from the *Z*ungarian desert to the confines of India. To the Moslem world his people were known as *K*ara-*k*itai (Black Cathayans).

In 1208 the Black Cathayan king gave shelter to the Turkic prince Küchlü*k* (ruler of the Naiman tribe) who had juſt been defeated by Chingiz Khan. Recently a

[1] The chronology is very uncertain; Moslem sources give the date of his death as 1143 (Journal Asiatique, 1920, p. 151).

vassal of the Cathayans, Alā-al-din Muhammed (Shah of Khwārizm), had asserted his independence. Küchlük now conspired with Muhammed against the Black Cathayan kingdom. Muhammed captured Samarkand in 1209; the last Cathayan monarch himself was captured by Küchlük in 1211.

The Kin Empire

We have seen that the Kin Tartars captured Peking in 1123. In 1127 they captured K'ai-fēng Fu, the capital of the Sungs, who retired beyond the Yangtze and set up a new capital at Hangchow. The Kins continued to rule from Peking where their government was supported by such of the Kitai as had remained behind. By a treaty signed in 1141 the Kins were allotted the provinces of Chihli, Shansi, Shantung, most of Honan and Shensi, with a small part of Kiangnan.

The Conquests of Chingiz Khan

It is not necessary to give here a full account of Chingiz Khan's career, more particularly as Vladimirtsov's excellent book on the subject has now appeared in English.[1] It will be sufficient to remind the reader that he was born in 1155 or 1156. It was not till 1206 (that is to say, in his fifty-ninth or sixtieth year) that, by a series of campaigns, he succeeded in uniting under his rule the various Mongol and Turkic

[1] Routledge, 6s.

tribes. It was on this occasion that he was proclaimed Ocean-great Khan.[1] He then conquered successively the Tanguts and the Kin Tartars, his generals capturing Peking in 1215. While the Mongol armies steadily advanced in China, Chingiz himself turned west and attacked the former empire of the Black Cathayans. By 1218 he was master of Turkestan. He then fell upon Muhammed, who had inherited the more westerly portion of the Cathayan empire. Samarkand fell in May, 1220. Already a year before this Chingiz had sent his first summons to the Taoist Ch'ang-ch'un.

CHINGIZ AND MONGOL RELIGION

Buddhism did not begin to spread among the Mongols until after their conquest of Northern China. Their native religion was to a great extent derived (and this is true of all such culture as they possessed) from the Turks, who in turn had borrowed partly from the Iranians and partly from the Avars.[2] This religion consisted in the veneration of fire and of river-spirits, together with a belief in an indefinite sky-power (*Tängri*, Heaven). There was no regular priesthood, but certain persons were supposed to be in communication with Heaven and hence to derive magical powers

---

[1] M. Pelliot regards " Chingiz " as a palatalized form of the Turkic " tengiz ", " ocean ". The title is thus parallel to that of the Dalai Lama ; for " dalai " means " ocean " in Mongol.

[2] Predecessors of the Turks in the domination of Mongolia.

4

of prophecy, rain-making, and the like. These were called *bögä*, " wizards ", which, like *Tängri*, is a word of Turkish origin.

With one of these visionaries, a certain " sign-lord "[1] (reader of omens) called Kökchü, Chingiz came into conflict at an early period in his career, and it is possible that this experience may to some extent have alienated him from the national religion. But his successive patronage of Buddhism and Taoism was, I think, chiefly due to a belief that a great monarch should be supported by an equally great sage.

Possibly the story of Alexander and Aristotle—so widely spread throughout the East, was not unknown to him. A certain amount of trade was carried on in Mongolia by Moslem pedlars, and the Mongols were thus, even before the days of their expansion, not entirely cut off from the Mohammedan world.[2]

Chingiz and the Buddhists

European writers have in general given the impression that the patronage of the Mongols was extended

---

[1] *Täb-tängri. Tängri* does not here mean " Heaven," but is a mere title of respect. A " knower of heavenly signs ", belonging to the same tribe as Kökchü, gave the future Emperor Mongka his name in 1208, and it has been assumed that Kökchü's revolt was subsequent to this. It is not however certain that Mongka's name-giver was the same person as Kökchü. The story of the revolt as given in the *Secret History* (ch. xii) is obviously to some extent legendary. Thus we are told that Kökchü's family never again enjoyed power or credit ; but we learn from the *Yüan Shih* (ch. 193, life of Pai-pa) that Kökchü's brother Torin held the intimate Court post of *chärbi* (chamberlain).

[2] According to tradition there was a Moslem leader (Ja'afar Khoja) in the Khan's army so early as 1206 ; but these accounts of Chingiz's early followers are largely legendary.

only to the magical and ritualistic form of Buddhism which had its home in Tibet. This, for the early reigns is by no means true. It was indeed not to Tibetan Buddhism but to its extreme opposite, the native Chinese Meditation[1] Sect, that the Mongols first felt drawn. The following account, though drawn from Buddhist sources, has every right to be regarded as historical.

Hai-yün

The Zen priest Hai-yün was born in 1202. When the Mongols overran Shansi in 1214 he was living at Lan-ch'ēng in Shansi with his aged master Chung-kuan, and his biographer[2] tells us that on this occasion Hai-yün met the great Khan. This however is improbable, for Chingiz was not with the army that invaded Shansi. This army was led by the Khan's sons Kasar, Chagatai and Ögödäi and it was probably one of these younger Khans whom Hai-yün met in 1214.

---

[1] Chinese, Ch'an. Sanskrit, Dhyāna. But generally known to Europeans by its Japanese name, Zen. Dhyāna figures as one of the chief forms of religious practice at all periods of Buddhist history. The Chinese sect, however, specialized in this one form of practice almost to the exclusion of others. The pious activity of its own historians has wrapped the origins of this sect in a cloud of fable. Fresh light on the question is afforded by Dr. Hu Shih's recent edition of the newly-discovered works of the seventh Patriarch, Shēn-hui.

[2] Ch'ang-nien, author of the Fo Tsu Li Tai T'ung Tsai, 1323. See H. Kunishita: "Relations of the Early Mongol Emperors with the Buddhist priests of the Dhyāna Sect", Tōyō Gakuhō, XI, 4 and XII, 1 (in Japanese). For the passage in Ch'ang-nien, see Takakusu, Vol. 49, p. 702, col. 2.

INTRODUCTION

In 1219, at the time of the third campaign against the Kin Tartars, Shansi was again overrun. The population of Lan-ch'ēng fled in panic. On entering the town, Shih T'ien-hsiang, a northern Chinese who had taken service with the Mongol general Mukali, was surprised to meet a young Zen priest going about in complete unconcern. T'ien-hsiang asked him whether he was not afraid of the soldiers. " Not at all ", said Hai-yün ; " I have confidence in them as protectors of the Faith[1] ". This answer pleased Shih T'ien-hsiang and, continuing the conversation, another general, a certain Li Ch'i-ko who was also a Chinese in the service of the Mongols, and therefore acquainted with the divisions of contemporary Buddhism, asked Hai-yün whether he was a follower of Zen or of the Doctrines.[2] Hai-yün answered that he regarded these two branches of religion as equally important. " They are ", he said, " like the two wings of a bird or like warriors and scholars, with neither of whom a State can dispense ". Hai-yün then introduced them to his master, Chung-kuan, whose doctrine pleased them so much that they enrolled themselves as his disciples. The Mongol general Mukali also interested himself on the priests' behalf and sent a report concerning them direct to the Great Khan. The following answer from

[1] Lit.: " outside protectors ", a term applied to secular champions of Buddhism, as opposed to " inner protectors ", i.e. the discipline of the Faith itself.
[2] i.e. of the T'ien-t'ai or of the Tantric Sect.

7

Chingiz was brought by his chamberlains Taisu-buka and Ma-lai : " From what your messengers have told me it appears that the old Reverend One, and the young Reverend One are both true ' speakers to Heaven '. Feed and clothe them well, and if you find any others of the same sort gather them all in and let them ' speak to Heaven ' as much as they will. They are not to be treated with disrespect by any one and are to rank as ' darkan ' (Mongol freemen) ".[1]

Chung-kuan died next year (1220) ; Hai-yün, then aged eighteen, was too young to be considered seriously as a " speaker to Heaven ". It was now the turn of the Taoists to receive Imperial attention. But before describing the Khan's dealings with this religion, it will be well to give some account (since none has hitherto been available) of the sect to which Ch'ang-ch'un, Chingiz's next protegé, belonged ; and this account must necessarily be preceded by a few words on the Taoist religion in general.

Taoism

Europeans who have heard of Taoism associate it on the one hand with the mystic philosophy of Lao Tzŭ and Chuang Tzŭ, and on the other with a degraded pseudo-clergy that with its spells and charms trades on the superstition of the modern Chinese peasant. The history of Taoism during the two thousand years that

[1] Takakusu, Vol. 49, p. 703, col. 1.

lie between is entirely unknown to the general reader and has as yet been very little ftudied even by specialifts.

The ftrength of Taoism has consifted in the faĉt that, unlike Buddhism, it had a definite ecclesiaftical organization, controlled by an hereditary potentate whom the Chinese call the Heavenly Mafter and Europeans have usually called the Taoift Pope. This spiritual dynafty was founded by a certain Chang Tao-ling who in the middle of the second century A.D. received from a celeftial messenger a revelation of the " True and unique (*Chĕng-i*) Tao ". This myftery ftill remains in the possession of the Chang family, the present Pope being, I think, the sixty-third of his line. What Chang aĉtually did was to colleĉt the talismans, spells and charms of country witch-doĉtors and incorporate them for the firft time with a kind of religious syftem, founded on the teachings of Lao Tzŭ. Hitherto religion had meant to the Chinese a scattered congerie of inconsiftent cults and praĉtices. The notion of a religion as a set of beliefs grouped round the figure of a single founder had quite recently made its appearance with the introduĉtion of Buddhism. In the creation of Chang Tao-ling's new Taoism the influence of Buddhism probably counted for something.[1]

[1] In another part of China—the Soochow diftriĉt—about a hundred years later a certain Yû Chi played much the same part as Chang Tao-ling in the weft. In his case however the influence of Buddhism was much more apparent. Unlike that of Chang Tao-ling his seĉt did not survive him.

INTRODUCTION

The great service rendered by the new Church was that it became a depository of texts and doctrines which Confucianism rejected as heterodox; of philosophic doctrines on the one hand, and of the sciences and pseudo-sciences (astrology, alchemy, hygiene, phototherapy, divination, sex-determination, etc.) on the other. Had it not been for the competition of Buddhism, all would have been well. The Buddhists had the immense advantage of continually drawing from the inexhaustible stocks of Indian theology fresh supplies of dogma and discipline. The creative faculty of the Taoists was quite unable to keep pace with this torrent of importations. From the fifth century onwards the Taoists produced a long succession of scriptures slavishly modelled on those of their rivals. At the same time[1] they began to elaborate an iconography modelled on that of Buddhism. Lao Tzŭ here figures as a counterpart to Śākyamuni, the historic Buddha; T'ien Tsun (the Heaven-honoured One, which is in itself one of the ten appellations of Buddha) corresponds more or less to Amitabha, and a host of *chēn-jēn*[2] (" perfected men ") play the part of the Buddhist Bodhisattvas. Lao Tzŭ was, moreover, like Buddha, provided both retrospectively and prophetically with countless incarnations. Needless to say,

[1] The earliest surviving dated image of a Taoist deity bears, according to Dr Tokiwa (*Tōyō Gakutō* X, 2, 327), the date 513.
[2] This is the term that I have usually translated " Adept ".

Taoism also imitated the temples, feſtivals and
monaſtic life of its competitors.

But in one branch of ſtudy the Taoiſts were unique.
To them alone is due the vaſt body of alchemical
literature, which makes the Chinese sources more
important than even the Mohammedan to the hiſtorian
of this ſtrange subjeƈt. The Chinese had inherited
from the remote paſt the belief that certain subſtances
such as jade, pearl, mother-of-pearl, cinnabar, were life-
giving, and that if absorbed into the body they would
prevent the gradual deteriorations of old age. As they
exiſt in nature, however, these subſtances, it was
thought, are always " impure ". Only when made
artificially can they be safely and efficaciously ingeſted.
In early China gold was not highly valued. When
through contaƈt with the gold-prizing nomads of the
north-weſt the Chinese, in the three or four centuries
before the Chriſtian era, began to accept gold as their
higheſt ſtandard of value, the ideas previously attached
to other " life-giving " and consequently valuable
subſtances became associated also with gold. Thus
arose various diſtinƈt forms of alchemy : (1) the
attempt to produce a liquid gold that could be
drunk and so produce longevity ; (2) the so-called
" Gold-cinnabar " alchemy. To the recipes for
making artificial cinnabar and thus producing an elixir
of life was arbitrarily added the further clause that

" when the cinnabar is made, gold will easily follow ".
We thus see the new life-giving substance gold tagged
on to the beliefs connected with the older substance,
cinnabar. (3) An attempt, parallel to that of the
earliest Western alchemy, to produce gold from baser
metals such as lead.

The earliest extant Chinese treatises on alchemy are
contained in the writings of Pao P'u Tzŭ[1], who
distinguishes clearly between the three forms of
alchemy mentioned above. A number of still earlier
books on the subject were known to Pao P'u Tzŭ, and
it is clear that an alchemy of gold existed in China at
least as early as the first century B.C. That this
particular sort of alchemy (the only one to which
we in Europe apply the term) existed in very early
times in China is impossible; for importance was not
then attached to gold. But we have every reason
to suppose that the artificial production of other
substances, such as jade, went on from the earliest
days.

Often in the alchemical literature of the Renaissance
and later we have a suspicion that we are reading not
about material experiments, but about a spiritual quest
allegorically described in terms of the laboratory. In
China this suspicion is a certainty. From the tenth
century onwards exoteric alchemy (*wai tan*) gives place

[1] The philosophical pseudonym of Ko Hung, fourth century.

INTRODUCTION

to esoteric (*nei tan*[1]), which inftead of using tangible and material fubftances as its ingredients, uses only the " souls " or " essences " of these fubftances. These " souls " are the " true " or purified mercury, sulphur, lead, etc., and are in the same relation to common metals as is the Taoift, Adept or *Chēn-jēn* (purified, perfected man), to ordinary mortals. By the end of the eleventh century a fresh ftep has been made. These transcendental metals are identified with various parts of the human body, and alchemy comes to mean in China not an experimentation with chemicals, blow-pipes, furnace and the like (though these survive in the popular alchemy of itinerant quacks), but a fyftem of mental and physical re-education. It was in this sense that Ch'ang-ch'un, whose travels are here recorded, was an alchemift, and it is a myfticism of this kind that is expounded in his " Straight Guide to the Mighty Elixir[2]".

But before describing Ch'ang-ch'un's own doctrines and career, we muft ftudy the hiftory of the peculiar sect to which he belonged.

The Ch'üan-chēn Sect

Wang Chē, the founder of the sect, was born in 1112. In 1159, when walking by the Kan-ho (Sweet River) in the Chung-nan Mountains near Hsi-an Fu, he fell

---

[1] The *nei tan* or esoteric elixir is, however, already mentioned by the Buddhift writer Hui-ssŭ (b. 515; d. 577). See Takakusu, Vol. 46, p. 791, col. 3.
[2] *T'ai Tan Chih-chih*. Wieger's catalogue, No. 241.

13

in with two mysterious strangers from whom he received the revelation of the Ch'üan-chēn doctrine. In 1161 he immured himself in a grave ten feet deep, where he remained for two years. Emerging in 1163 he built himself a hut where he remained in solitary meditation till 1167, when he suddenly set fire to it and was found dancing about amid the ashes. Hospitality was then given to him at Ning-hai by a certain Ma Yü, who built him a retreat in a corner of his garden. This hut was called Ch'üan-chēn, that is "completely sublimated"; hence the name of the sect which Wang Chē founded. Here, in self-imposed confinement, he remained in one room for the greater part of 1168. Ma Yü and his wife were both converted and became important figures in the new sect. In 1169 he moved to the Golden Lotus Hall at Ning-hai, whence the alternative name of his sect, which is often called the Chin Lien (Golden Lotus). Here he founded the Golden Lotus Congregation of the Three Doctrines, the first of a number of religious associations founded by him in the last years of his life. The three doctrines were those of Confucius's disciple Tzŭ Ssŭ, as expressed in the *Chung Yung* ("Doctrine of the Mean", or so-called by its English translators); of Bodhidharma, the legendary founder of the Zen sect; and of Lao Tzŭ as expressed in the *Tao Tē Ching*. He died in 1170, appointing Ch'ang-ch'un as his successor.

INTRODUCTION

"Wang Chē", says Hsiang-mai,[1] "distinguished himself more by his eccentricity than by his sanctity ". He was indeed known as "Wang the Madman ". But before considering what ideas inspired his peculiar conduct, we will examine the career of his equally eccentric disciple, Ho Kuang-ning. Ho was born in 1140. Becoming a Taoist of the Fakir-like school which Wang Chē had founded, he stationed himself in 1175 on the bridge at Wu-chou, where he remained night and day without moving. He ate only when food was given to him and betrayed no emotion when taunted or jostled by passers-by. Here he remained for three years, till one day a drunk man bumped into him and sent him flying over the side of the bridge. It was noticed that he had disappeared, but no one troubled to look for him, and it was assumed that he had at last tired of his pitch. After some while an official attempted to cross the bridge on horse-back. His horse shied and would not cross. The official was certain that something underneath the bridge was frightening the horse. A search was made and under the bridge, at the edge of the water, was found the holy Kuang-ning.

The people of the town were much distressed and begged him to resume his post on the bridge. But he remained exactly where he had fallen for three years.

[1] Author of the *Pien Wei Lu*, 1291 A.D.

15

INTRODUCTION

In 1182 he adopted a sort of Stylite-existence on a raised platform at Chēn-ting in Chihli, from which point of vantage he preached to vast audiences. He died in 1212.

Lastly, before considering the general characteristics of the sect, I will set down the main facts of Ch'ang-ch'un's career previous to 1219, when the narrative of the *Hsi Yu Chi* begins.

Born in 1148 Ch'ang-ch'un became a Taoist monk in 1166, studying in the K'un-lun mountains in Shantung. In 1167 he became a pupil of Wang Chē, the founder of the Completely Sublimated Sect, at Ning-hai.[1] In 1174 he moved to P'an-ch'i in Shensi province; then to Lung-chou, Lung-mēn Shan, and finally to the Chung-nan Mountains near the modern Hsi-an Fu.

By this time his reputation had spread far and wide over northern China. In 1188 he had an audience with Shih Tsung, the Kin Tartar Emperor of northern China. In 1191 he returned to Shangtung and lived at Ch'i-hsia, near Ning-hai.

In 1207 the Kin princess Yüan Fei presented the T'ai-hsü Kuan, the temple where Ch'ang-ch'un was living, with a complete copy of the Taoist Canon.

The rest of Ch'ang-ch'un's career is described in the *Hsi Yu Chi*, and does not here concern us.

[1] In Tēng-chou Fu, Shantung. On Wang Chē's death in 1170, Ch'ang-ch'un, as we have seen, became head of the sect.

INTRODUCTION

Li Chih-ch'ang

Li Chih-ch'ang, the author of the *Hsi Yu Chi*, was born in 1193. He became a pupil of Ch'ang-ch'un in 1218 and soon afterwards, as we shall see, accompanied him on his journey to the West. In 1227 when upon Ch'ang-ch'un's death, Yin Chih-p'ing became head of the sect, Li Chih-ch'ang became Registrar of the sect and Intendant of the Ch'ang-ch'un Temple. In 1229 he interviewed the new Emperor Ögödäi concerning the education of the Crown Prince. Li Chih-ch'ang explained his views upon the *Book of Poetry*, the *Book of History*, the *Tao Tê Ching* and *Book of Filial Piety*. The Emperor expressed his approval.

In 1230 information was given to the Government that the monks of the Ch'ang-ch'un Temple had decorated their walls with paintings which constituted an insult to Buddhism. These paintings, as we know from the *Pien Wei Lu*, represented the Eighty-one Incarnations of Lao Tzŭ, in which Buddha figures merely as one of the many guises assumed by Lao Tzŭ in his successive Births. Yin Chih-p'ing, the head of the sect, was seized ; but Li Chih-ch'ang, as Intendant of the Ch'ang-ch'un Temple, insisted upon assuming the sole responsibility. He was sentenced to await trial, and put in prison. His release, which followed shortly, was no doubt due to the intervention of some influential patron. But the

17

INTRODUCTION

pious narrative[1] of his biographer tells us that the chains which had been put upon him repeatedly burst of themselves. The gaoler, on going to inform the Governor of the prison, found him much upset; he was at breakfast, and upon every mouthful was dimly imprinted the image of this new prisoner, Li Chih-ch'ang. The case against the Taoists was at once dismissed.

In 1233 he was appointed tutor to the Mongol princes at Peking. Two years later he was ordered to build a Taoist temple at Karakorum.[2] In the many Imperial communications which he received at this time he was referred to, we are told, as Hsien K'ung Bagshi, "Professor of the doctrines of the *hsien* (i.e., of Taoism) and of Confucius".[3] In 1238 Yin Chih-p'ing (Ch'ang-ch'un's successor) retired and handed over the control of the sect to Li Chih-ch'ang. In 1251, on the accession of Mongka Khan, this appointment was confirmed. In 1253 it was decreed that all persons taking vows as Taoist monks or nuns must have their certificate stamped by Li Chih-ch'ang. In 1256 he retired, leaving the succession to Chang Chih-ch'ing. He died twenty-two years later, in 1278. Besides the

[1] His tomb-inscription, composed by Wang O; *Kan Shui Hsien Yüan Lu, III,* 14 recto (Wieger, 965).
[2] The new Mongol capital.
[3] This name, which occurs in an edict of 1235, puzzled Chavannes, who did not realize that it referred to Li Chih-ch'ang. See *T'oung Pao,* 1908, p. 308. K'ung may, however, not mean Confucius, but be simply a transcription of the Mongol word for "man".

INTRODUCTION

Hsi Yu Chi, he left a *Hsüan Chi* "Treaty on Profundi-
ties" in twenty chapters; this does not seem to survive.

What then were the principles of the sect founded
by Wang Chē and continued by Ch'ang-ch'un ?

The sect was distinguished, as we have already seen,
by a fanatical asceticism. Of Ch'ang-ch'un himself
we read that he took neither fruit nor tea. Yüan
Hao-wēn[1] tells us, moreover, that so far as possible the
followers of Wang Chē avoided sleep. "They call
this abstention 'smelting away the dark demon'.
There are now in the Capital some among them, who
have not lain down for ten years." Yin Chih-p'ing,
who accompanied Ch'ang-ch'un on his journey and
succeeded him as head of the sect, was also a great
advocate of sleeplessness. Several writers of the sect
lament the mutual hostility of Buddhists and Taoists,[2]
and according to Hsiang-mai[3] Ch'ang-ch'un claimed
to have broken down the barriers that divided the
three religions and shown that Taoism was the original
starting-point of both Confucianism and Buddhism.
In such a synthesis of the three religions Ch'ang-ch'un
was not attempting anything new, and we must look
elsewhere for any element of originality in the teachings
of the sect.

[1] 1190-1257. *Works*, XXXI.
[2] Especially a poem by Ma Yü (Wieger, Catalogue No. 1135, VIII, 23 verso)
beginning : "Taoists attack priests, priests attack Taoists. But we monks of either
persuasion had far better spend our time in attending to our 'natural self'".
[3] *Pien Wei Lu, III.*

INTRODUCTION

The Taoist Ch'u-li, writing in 1241,[1] tells us that Wang Chē, Ch'ang-ch'un's predecessor, devoted himself chiefly to the discussion of *hsing-ming*, a subject which during the preceding century (the eleventh) had only been treated in an imperfect way.

The term *hsing-ming* has a long history. Originally *hsing* meant the inborn qualities of a person or thing ; *ming*, his or its destiny as decreed by Heaven. But in the first half of the ninth century we find Li Ao, nephew by marriage of the celebrated Han Yü,[2] using *hsing* and *ming* as terms to denote a man's " natural state " as it exists before it becomes corrupted by the contacts of life ; and it is interesting that in a Chinese Manichean[3] hymn of about the same date, *hsing-ming* occurs as an equivalent to the North Aryan term *grev jivondogh*, " Living Self "—i.e., the portion of the Light Element that is imprisoned in the darkness of the body.

If the subject of the *hsing-ming* (natural state) and how it may best be kept free from pollution was, as Ch'u-li suggests, imperfectly understood, this was not for lack of attention. *Hsing-ming* was indeed one of the main topics of the Neo-Confucian School whose

[1] Preface to Wieger, 170.

[2] 768-824, the great writer whose onslaughts upon Buddhism and Taoism are well known to English readers. Cf. Giles, *History of Chinese Literature*, p. 200. For Li Ao's "Three Letters on the Restoration of the Natural State ", see " Complete Prose Works of the T'ang Dynasty ", Ch. 637, f. 14 verso.

[3] Stein MSS. from Tun-huang, S.2659. See Waldschmidt und Lenz. " Die Stellung Jesu im Manichäismus ", 1926.

philosophers, in a long line from Chou Tun-i (died 1073) to Chu Hsi (died 1200), taught with various modifications of Li Ao's doctrine how the "natural state" may be recaptured or preserved. But whereas the Ch'üan Chēn sect practised a rabid and inhuman asceticism, the Neo-Confucians advocated no more than a mildly Puritanical régime.[1]

For an exposition of Ch'ang-ch'un's tenets we naturally turn to the sermon[2] which he preached to Chingiz on November 19th, 1222. It begins as follows: Tao is the producer of Heaven and the nurturer of Earth. The sun and moon, the stars and planets, demons and spirits, men and things all grow out of Tao. Most men only know the greatness of Heaven; they do not understand the greatness of Tao. My sole object in living all my life separated from my family and in the monastic state has been to study this question.

When Tao produced Heaven and Earth, they in turn opened up and produced Man. When Man was first born he shone with a holy radiance of his own and his step was so light that it was as if he flew. The earth bore fungoids that were moist and sweet-tasting. Without waiting to roast or cook them, Man ate them all

---

[1] Ch'u-li in the same place mentions that Wang Chē altered the costume of his followers, giving them "patchwork jerkins". I have found no other reference to this.

[2] Published under the title *Hsüan Fēng Ch'ing Hui Lu* in 1232. Wieger, No.1410.

raw ; at this time nothing was cooked for eating. The fungoids were all sweet-smelling. Man with his nose smelt their scent and with his mouth taſted their taſte. Gradually his body grew heavy and his holy light grew dim.[1] This was because his appetite and longing were so keen. Those who ſtudy Tao muſt learn not to desire the things that other men desire, not to live in the places where other men live. They muſt do without pleasant sounds and sights, and get their pleasure only out of purity and quiet. They muſt rejeçt luscious taſtes and use foods that are fresh and light as their only delicacy. If there is any attachment (to concrete things) the follower of Tao will fail to underſtand it or its operations. If the eye sees pleasant sights or the ear hears pleasant sounds, if the mouth enjoys pleasant taſtes or the natural ſtate is perturbed by emotions, then the original Spirit is scattered and lost . . .

The male we call Yang ; his element is fire. The female we call Yin : her element is water. But Yin (the imperfeçt) can quench Yang (the perfeçt) ; water conquers fire. Therefore, the Taoiſt muſt above all abſtain from luſt. It is true that in providing himself with food and clothing a man expends a good deal of

[1] The ſtory of the proto-man and his dwindling light has a very Manichean ring about it ; but no exact parallel can be quoted. It is essentially the same ſtory as that of the Biblical Creation, but in a much simplified form. Cf. Von Wesendonk, *Urmensch und Seele*, 1924. For the contacts between Taoism and Manicheism see Chavannes and Pelliot : *Un Traité Manichéen*, 1911-1913. Particularly p. 289.

worry and fret, which leads to a loss of Original Spirit. But the loss in this case is quite small; whereas a licentious life waſtes the fine particles of the soul and leads to a considerable loss of original spirit. Tao (the original indifferentiated subſtance of life) split up into two forms. The one, light and pure. This became the sky. The sky is male and belongs to the element fire. The other form is heavy and unclean. This became earth. The earth is female and belongs to the element water.

Ch'ang-ch'un then explains how by nurturing in himself the element that is akin to heaven and checking the element that is akin to earth, " Man rises to Heaven and becomes a *hsien,* juſt as a flame goes upward. . . . If common people, who possess only one wife can ruin themselves by excessive indulgence, what must happen to monarchs, whose palaces are filled with concubines ? I learnt recently that Liu Wēn had been commissioned to search Peking and other places for women to fill your harem. Now I have read in the *Tao Tĕ Ching* that not to see things which arouse desire keeps the mind free from disorders. Once such things have been seen, it is hard indeed to exercise self-reſtraint. I would have you bear this in mind."

Ch'ang-ch'un then gives a short account (containing nothing that is new to us) of his early life and association with Ma Yü (1123-1183), Tan Ch'ang-chēn

INTRODUCTION

(1123-1185), and Liu Ch'ang-shēng (1150-1203). This is
followed by a sketch of Taoiſt hiſtory, and of the various
revelations vouchsafed to the patriarchs of the Church.

Now all people from Emperors and princes down
to the loweſt classes, however different their lives may
be in other ways, are alike in this, that they possess a
" natural ſtate ". All Emperors and monarchs are
heavenly beings who have been exiled from Heaven.
If they are virtuous on earth they will, on their return
to Heaven, be allotted a higher place than before.
Try, Ch'ang-Ch'un urges Chingiz, sleeping alone for
one month. You will be surprised what an improvement there will be in your spirits and energy. The
ancients said : " To take medicine for a thousand days
does less good than to lie alone for a single night ".
Chingiz has already produced a numerous poſterity
and can afford to husband his ſtrength.

It is however, when Ch'ang-ch'un turns from moral
to political advice that his discourse becomes intereſting.
He suggeſts that an honeſt and competent official with
knowledge of the whole queſtion should be sent to
China with inſtructions to work out a plan by which
the people of the northern provinces and Shantung,
long harassed by war, could be remitted taxation for
three years. Such a plan muſt of course provide for
some means of supporting the Mongol troops and
officials in occupation of these provinces. As a

precedent for the employment of a Chinese in the capacity of general agent for a foreign invader, Ch'ang-ch'un quotes the case of Liu Yü, who, while the feelings of the Chinese towards the Kin Tartar invaders was ftill uncertain, was set up as "Emperor of the Ch'i dynaſty "[1] and in eight years had completely accuſtomed the people to the idea of foreign rule.

Ch'ang-ch'un does not mention any one in particular as suitable for such a rôle ; but it is probable that he had some Shantung patron in mind.

Laſtly, he recounts the success of his methods in the case of another Imperial personage, the Kin Emperor Shih Tsung,[2] whom as we have already seen, he interviewed in 1188. This monarch's debauches had reduced him to such a pitiable condition that he could only totter to his morning Audiences with two men holding him up, one on each side. Aċting on the same advice as Ch'ang-ch'un gave to Chingiz, the Kin Emperor " completely recovered his ſtrength and aċtivity ". Ch'ang-ch'un, somewhat disingenuously, does not mention that his interview with Shih Tsung took place in 1188 and that by 1189 the monarch was dead. The improvement in his health was evidently of a very temporary nature.

---

[1] At first (1130) with his Capital at Ta-ming in Chihli; later at K'ai-fēng in Honan. In 1137 the Tartars, having no further use for Liu Yü, deposed him and took his domains under their direċt control. He was executed in 1146.

[2] Born 1122 ; died 1189.

INTRODUCTION

Up to the time of Ch'ang-ch'un it was by its extreme asceticism that the Ch'üan-chēn sect chiefly impressed the outer world. In this connection it may be worth while to mention a contemporary sect which seems to have devoted itself to similar practices.

In the *Works* of Yeh-lü Ch'u-ts'ai we find frequent references to a sect called Dhuta,[1] which had apparently obtained a very wide hold over the lower classes in the second quarter of the thirteenth century. Ch'u-ts'ai regards the Dhūta-ism as a Buddhist heresy ; but the Mongol government counted it as a separate religion.[2] To their enemies the Dhūta-ists were known as " Husk-pests " (*k'ang-nieh*), a name the origin of which has not, I think, been explained.

The fact that the Mongols ranked them as an independent religious unit, on a par with the Christians, Moslems and Manicheans, shows that the Dhūta-ists deserve more attention than they have at present received. Yeh-lü Ch'u-ts'ai's denunciations of them have not hitherto been noticed.

TAOIST INDISCRETIONS

Ch'ang-ch'un and Yeh-lü Ch'u-ts'ai

Even during the life-time of Ch'ang-ch'un the Taoists seem to have made a very indiscreet use of

[1] Ascetic.
[2] See Pelliot, *Bulletin de l'École d'Extrême-Orient*, iii, 315, IV. 438, and *T'oung Pao*, 1922, p. 351.

INTRODUCTION

the favour which their master's prestige had secured for them. Beginning by appropriating Buddhist monasteries that had fallen into decay during the recent campaigns, they went on to seize (or were accused by their rivals of seizing) a long series of fully-occupied and flourishing Buddhist monasteries; they were also accused of destroying Buddhist images and systematically replacing them by images of Lao Tzŭ and other Taoist divinities.

The first protest raised against these excesses is contained in the *Hsi Yu Lu*[1] of Yeh-lü Ch'u-ts'ai (1190 to 1244 A.D.), which was published in 1229, only two years after Ch'ang-ch'un's death

Yeh-lü Ch'u-ts'ai, a descendant of the Cathayan (*K*itai) royal family, was Governor of Peking at the time (1215) of its capture by the Mongols. The Cathayans were by race closely allied to the Mongols and received preferential treatment. Yeh-lü Ch'u-ts'ai became Chingiz Khan's Chinese secretary and for more than thirty years constituted the principal link between the Mongols and Chinese culture. He confesses[2] that " in his youth " (he was thirty-two at the time when he associated with Ch'ang-ch'un at Samarkand) he had been led away by the doctrines of the Ch'üan Chen

---

[1] This book was till 1927 known only in quotations. It was probably suppressed by Ch'u-ts'ai's son Yeh-lü Chu, who was an ardent Taoist. Recently it turned up in Japan and was published by Prof. Kanda Ki-ichirō. I have, however, failed to procure it.

[2] See Wang Kuo-wei's edition of the *Hsi Yu Chi*, I, 35, verso, l. 6.

Taoist sect. His poetical works contain forty-four pieces written " to the rhymes " of poems by Ch'ang-ch'un[1]. It is natural to suppose that at the time when these pieces were made he was on good terms with the sage. The last of them was written on March 9th, 1222, the day when " the officials invited the Master to take a walk to the West of the town ".

On November 19th of the same year Yeh-lü Ch'u-ts'ai, as part of his secretarial duties, was obliged to write down, and, no doubt, to put into final literary form, one of the Master's discourses. To this work he prefixed, as he was bound to do, a short note (five lines) describing the circumstances under which the discourse was delivered. There is nothing in these lines to indicate either partiality or hostility to Ch'ang-ch'un's doctrines. The *Pien Wei Lu*[2] says that on this occasion Yeh-lü Ch'u-ts'ai was asked whether he would care to compose a verse-eulogy summarizing Ch'ang-ch'un's speech : " The Secretary (Yeh-lü Ch'u-ts'ai) maintained a scornful silence ; but those who were in the know were convulsed with amusement at such an idea ". But this book was composed in 1291, long after the events, and the discredit of Taoism is its sole aim, so that such an anecdote as the above is

[1] This fact was discovered by Wang Kuo-wei. In every case Yeh-lü Ch'u-ts'ai has obliterated Ch'ang-ch'un's name, either saying " Written to the rhymes of some one else ", or substituting some quite different name.

[2] III, 29 verso of the Kyōto Tripitaka. Takakusu, Vol. 52, p. 766, col. 2. See above, pp. 15 and 19.

not necessarily to be believed. We have indeed no reason to think that the quarrel began until outbreak of Taoiſt violence and intolerance after Ch'ang-ch'un's return to Peking in 1224. The cessation of literary amenities may only have meant that after March, 1222 the sage and the secretary were no longer living in daily contaćt. The discourse[1] recorded by Yeh-lü Ch'u-ts'ai on November 19th, 1222, was published in 1232. But there is no reason to suppose that this publication was instigated or sanctioned by Yeh-lü Ch'u-ts'ai himself or that it marks a ſtage in his controversy with the Taoiſt Church.

EVENTS AFTER CHA'NG-CH'UN'S DEATH

The Rivalry between Taoism and Buddhism

We know from the *Fo Tsu* . . . *T'ung Tsai* that soon after his ascent to the throne Güyük issued a proclamation (1247) appointing Hai-yün, who had now reached the respectable age of forty-five, to be the official head of Buddhism. At the same time the Khan's brother Karajar invited the Maſter to reside in Karakorum. The next Khan, Mongka, soon after his accession (1251) confirmed this appointment and at the same time made Li Chih-ch'ang, author of the *Hsi Yu Chi*, head of the whole Taoiſt Church. In 1252 we get the firſt intimation that the Mongols were discovering the

[1] See above, p. 21.

INTRODUCTION

exiftence of a type of Buddhism far better suited to their
ftate of culture than Chinese Zen. In this year the
Zen Buddhiſt Hai-yün is displaced, as head of the
religion, by Na-mo, a Tibetan[1] prieſt. The superior
attractions of Tibetan Buddhism, with its large
admixture of pagan devil-worship and magic, had been
discovered by Güyük's brother *K*adan, during his
residence in Szechuan. The signal for an aĉtual
outbreak of hoſtility between Buddhiſts and Taoiſts
was the arrival at *K*arakorum in 1255 of emissaries from
Li Chih-ch'ang who began distributing two books
called " Diagrams of the Eighty-one Incarnations of
Lao Tzŭ ", and " The Scripture of Lao Tzu's Converting the Barbarians and becoming Buddha ".[2] These
works were considered insulting to Buddhism, because
they represented Buddha as poſterior to Lao Tzŭ, and

[1] In the anti-Taoiſt ſtele-inscription of 1284 he is called Lan-ma and said to be
a native of Chi-pin. In the thirteenth century no country of Chi-pin any longer
exiſted and the expression (which is a literary archaism) may mean either Kashmir
(as in the Han dynaſty) or Kapiśa (as in the T'ang dynaſty).

If however Na-mo is identical with the Karma of Gigs-med-nam-mk'a's Mongol
hiſtory (Huth's translation, p. 136), he was to all intents and purposes a Tibetan.
Karma is ſtated to have lived from 1203 to 1282 and to have been summoned by
the Emperor Mongka (1251-1259). He was a pupil of the famous Tibetan prieſt
Sa-skhya, who obtained an influence over *K*adan Khan in Szechuan. Finally, the
Yüan Shih (ch. 125, f. 9, verso) mentions a zealous Buddhist called Na-mo, a native
of Kashmir, who attached himself to the Court of Ögödäi (1229-1244), conscious
that "his own country was about to collapse in the general upheaval which was
overwhelming the world " and scenting " an Imperial feeling in the air towards the
North-Eaſt ". This Na-mo is almoſt certainly the same person.

[2] To trace the hiſtory of these books would take us too far afield. Suffice it to
say that the " Scripture of Lao Tzŭ's conversions ", though frequently suppressed
by successive governments, had been exasperating the Buddhiſts by its continual
re-appearance ever since the sixth century. The Manicheans had now given it a
fresh lease of life by inserting in it a passage according to which, in one of his
incarnations, Lao Tzŭ was their founder, Mani.

indeed as having been merely one of the numerous incarnations of Lao Tzŭ. There were complaints concerning the circulation of these books by Li Chih-ch'ang, and the attention of the Emperor was finally called to the matter by his brother Ārik̠-bögä. Li Chih-ch'ang was ordered to appear before the Emperor and uphold the authenticity of these works in disputation with the Zen prieſt Fu-yu. The result was unfavourable to the Taoiſts and on the 29th day of the ninth month, 1255, the Emperor issued from his camp on the Kun-nor (south of the Kalotai-nor) an ediÂŽt[1] authorizing an enquiry into the charge of printing and circulating "false" scriptures. If it could be shown that Taoiſts had also, as alleged, deſtroyed Buddhiſt images and replaced them by Taoiſt ones, they were to make good this damage. But if a similar charge could be proved againſt the Buddhiſts, they likewise muſt make retribution.

The Taoiſts did not, it seems, amend their ways. There were fresh complaints and in 1256 another disputation took place, with numerous representatives on either side. No decision was reached, and it was decided that the dispute should recommence in the winter. On the appointed day the Taoiſts failed to appear.

During 1257 further complaints came from the

[1] Translated by Chavannes, *T'oung Pao*, 1904, p. 377, No. III.

INTRODUCTION

Buddhists, and Mongka, wearying of these perpetual wranglings,[1] handed the whole business over to his brother *K*ubilai. In 1258 a huge assemblage of disputants was collected at Shang-tu,[2] *K*ubilai's new residence. This time Confucians were also invited to attend, to the further discomfiture of the Taoists, who were convicted of stealing their doctrines from them as well as from the Buddhists. Seventeen prominent Taoists were forced to become Buddhist monks,[3] forty-five "forged scriptures" were ordered to be burnt and 237 Buddhist temples, which had been taken possession of by the Taoists, were returned to their former owners. I will not here trace in detail the further fluctuations of the conflict. A turning-point came in 1281, when it was proved that the Taoists had set fire to one of their own buildings in order to compromise the Buddhists by accusing them of incendiarism. The enquiry following on this accusation led to the edict of 1281,[4] which decreed the burning of all Taoist books except the *Tao Tĕ Ching*.

How far this decree was carried out, it is impossible

---

[1] Religious disputations seem, however, to have been his principal distraction. In 1254 the Minorite friar William of Rubruck took part in a great triangular contest between Christians, Mahommedans and Buddhists, and amid the plaudits of the first two parties, demonstrated to a Buddhist monk the existence of God. See *Sinica Franciscana*, p. 291.

[2] Coleridge's Xanadu, N.W. of the modern Dolon-nor.

[3] The Buddhists had suggested that the winners should behead the losers; *K*ubilai, shocked at this savagery, made the more civilized proposal that the defeated party should accept its opponent's religion.

[4] See *T'oung Pao*, 1904, p. 395, No. VII.

to say. It represented, in any case, a considerable
check to Taoism, and at no subsequent period in
Chinese history did this religion ever regain the
dominating position it held in the first half of the
thirteenth century. But despite a tendency towards
Tantric Buddhism, the Mongol Court did not abandon
its tolerance of " speakers to Heaven ", whatever might
be their creed ; and there is a decree of the Emperor
Wu-tsung, dated 1310, which bestows upon Ch'ang-
ch'un a posthumous title of the most sonorous and
impressive description.

Chinkai, the Leader of Ch'ang-ch'un's escort

The following account of Chinkai's life is to some
extent hypothetical. He seems to have been born in
1171. In 1203 he " drank the waters of the Baljiuna
river " with Chingiz Khan and was present at the
assembly on the Onon River in 1206.[1] During the
campaign against the Naimans Chingiz presented him
with one of his own horses. During the campaign
against the Kara-kitai he was rewarded for his services
by the gift of a banner decorated with marvellous
pearls and allowed to carry the Golden Tiger Tally.
He was ordered to found a colony of artizans and
craftsmen near the Argun Mountains (see below
p. 73), and the place was called after him " The City

[1] The legendary character of these early episodes has already been noticed, p. 5
(note).

33

of Chinkai ". In 1212 he took part in the campaign against the Kin Tartars and at the siege of Fu-chou went on fighting despite an arrow-wound in his left arm. After the capture of Peking in 1215 he climbed the Tower of the Great Compassionate One and shot four arrows, one in each direction. Chingiz allowed him to keep for his own, within the range of these arrows, whatever houses or lands most took his fancy. Ögödäi, the successor of Chingiz, made him chief Secretary of State and gave him control over all business conducted (as were the affairs of Turkestan and the western countries) in higher writing, and no official documents of any kind were considered legal unless, next to the date, they bore a confirmation written in Uighur letters by Chinkai. In 1232 he was present at the siege of K'ai-fēng, and in recognition of his services was given a Nine Dragon Banner and the right to use a sedan-chair. Next year he distinguished himself at the capture of Ts'ai-chou in Honan, and was made overlord of a thousand families in the city of Ēn-chou, in Shantung, the right to receive the taxes of these families being accorded to him and his descendants. A large colony of artizans and craftsmen which had previously existed at Hung-chou was now augmented by workers from Turkestan and K'ai-fēng, and the whole establishment placed under the control of Chinkai and his heirs.

34

INTRODUCTION

Ögödäi, the second Khan, died in 1242. During the regency of his widow Chinkai suffered an eclipse, but Güyük,[1] the third Khan, reſtored him to his former place and owing to the new Khan's ill-health almoſt the whole weight of government fell upon Chinkai and his colleague Kadak.

Güyük died in 1248. An attempt was made to place on the throne Ögödäi's grandson Shirämön. It was unsuccessful and eventually Mongka, a son of Chingiz Khan's brother Tuluï, became fourth Khan in 1251. Chinkai had supported the candidature of Shirämön, and in 1251, or early in 1252, he and Kadak, who had taken the same side, were both executed.

The tribe to which Chinkai belonged had been converted to Chriſtianity early in the eleventh century. Both Rashid and Juwaini speak of Chinkai as a Chriſtian.[2] Shirämön's mother was a Chriſtian and his own name is almoſt certainly a transcription of Solomon ; Chinkai himself loſt his life in an attempt to place a Chriſtian Khan upon the throne. The Moslem writers and two Chinese sources say that he was an Uighur. Owing to the prevalence of Chriſtianity among the Uighurs the Mohammedans often use the term Uighur merely in the sense of Chriſtian. Such a confusion is less

[1] The Minorite Brother Plano Carpini, sent by Innocent IV with letters to the Khan, arrived in time for Güyük's coronation, on Auguſt 24th, 1246. Here he encountered " Chingay ", whom he calls the Khan's " Protonotarius ". *Sinica Franciscana*, 119 and 123.
[2] So too Bar Hebræus, in his *Historia Dynastiarum*.

explicable in China, and I must discuss the rather complicated question of Chinkai's origins in an additional note.

Chinkai's Origins

The *Hei-ta Shih Luo*[1] says that Ögödäi had four Ministers, among whom "Chinkai, a Hui-hui, has special charge of Hui-hui affairs ". The term Hui-hui generally means Moslem, but is also used in the sense of " native of Turkestan ".

The *Mēng-ta Pei-lu*[2] says that in the early years of the thirteenth century there was a certain native of Turkestan with the surname T'ien who had acquired enormous wealth by commerce. This man had travelled about a great deal in Shantung and northern China. He described to the Mongols the richness of these lands and as his account coincided with that of some levies who had revolted against the rulers of northern China and joined the Mongols, it was decided to make an attack on the border provinces of northern China.

Now we know that Chinkai also bore the surname T'ien (" Field, Colony "), which (says his grave-inscription, composed by Hsü Yu-jēn[3]) was used in order to distinguish him from two other persons who

[1] Fol. 1 verso.
[2] Fol. 11 verso.
[3] Born 1287; died 1364. His *works* are contained in the *Chung-chou Ming-hsien Wên piao* of Liu Ch'ang (preface 1471). See also *Yüan Wên Lei* XXII, fol. 1.

bore the name Chin*k*ai. It is indeed as " Lord T'ien " that he is mo&t often referred to in Ch'ang-ch'un's *Travels*. Wang Kuo-wei sugge&ts that this Uighur merchant T'ien is identical with Chin*k*ai ; he also advances two further arguments for believing that, though Chin*k*ai is later qualified as a Kerait, he did not originally belong to the tribe. These reasons are :

(1) Chin*k*ai was present at the " drinking of the waters of the Baljiuna River ". This took place before the subjugation of the Keraits, and it is unlikely that we should find a Kerait fighting at so early a date on Chingiz's side. Wang Kuo-wei's argument, however, is that if Chin*k*ai was not a Kerait, we can accept the Moslem assertion that he was an Uighur. This seems to me a very &trange piece of reasoning. The Uighurs did not submit till long after the Keraits, and according to Wang's argument we should be &till more a&tonished at finding an Uighur in the Mongol army.

(2) In Ch'ang-ch'un's *Travels* (see below, p. 83) we are told that when the party reached Chambali*g* Chin*k*ai was greeted by the Uighur ruler of the place, " who was an old friend of his ". The conne&tion, however, between Chin*k*ai and the ruler of Chambali*g* was not that they were both Uighurs, but that they were both Chri&tians.[1]

---

[1] For the Chri&tian community at Chambali*g* in the thirteenth and fourteenth centuries, see Pelliot, *Journal Asiatique*, 1914, p. 497-498.

There seems to me, in short, to be no evidence that Chinkai was an Uighur. But there is reason to suppose that he had connections of some sort with Turkestan. It is singular to find a native of Mongolia sufficiently versed in western affairs to be put in charge of all foreign business. One would certainly have expected a native of Turkestan to be chosen for such a post. Doubts of this kind certainly existed in the minds of his Chinese admirers, for Hsü Yu-jēn in the above-quoted work, says that according to some accounts " Chinkai's original surname was T'ien, and it was only after his arrival in Mongolia that he became a member of the Kerait tribe ".

This, of course, is inconsistent with the theory that the surname T'ien was given in allusion to the colony that he organized *after* his arrival in Mongolia.

Liu wēn

Liu Wēn, often known as Liu Chung-lu, who figures so frequently in this narrative, originally entered the Khan's services as a herbalist. He also was renowned for his skill in making " singing arrows ". It was he, apparently,[1] who told Chingiz that Ch'ang-ch'un was three hundred years old and could teach others to live to a like age. Finally from the monograph on Rivers and Canals in the *Yuan Shih*[2] we learn

[1] See *Pien Wei Lu*, III, fol. 29 verso.
[2] *Yuan Shih*, ch. 64, 5 recto.

38

that in 1235 he was ordered to take charge of two hundred water-navvies who were to work on the Kerulen River in Eastern Mongolia.

A-li-hsien

The I-li-chi of the *History of the Kin Tartars*, the A-la-ch'ien of the *Yüan Shih*. He was a Tangut. The Mongols had, previous to the journey of Ch'ang-ch'un, employed him on numerous missions to the Kin Tartars from 1214 onwards.

History of the Text

The *Hsi Yu Chi* was incorporated in the Taoist Canon, but it remained quite unknown to the general public till it was published by Chang Mu in the well-known collection of texts called *Lien-yün-i Ts'ung-shu* (1848). To the learned world the existence of the book had been known since 1791, when the scholar Ch'ien Ta-hsin called attention to the importance of the book as a source for the history and geography of the early Mongol period. The Russian orthodox missionary, Palladius, translated the book into Russian, and Bretschneider gave in Vol. I of his Medieval Researches what is in effect a somewhat inaccurate abridgment of the Russian translation, furnished how-ever with an annotation that is often valuable.

39

INTRODUCTION

Of the numerous Chinese commentaries on the book I will mention only that of Wang Kuo-wei, now included in the collected edition of his works[1]; "le commentaire de W.", writes M. Pelliot, " par sa richesse, rejette dans l'ombre tous ceux qui l'ont précédé ".

Important, however, as Wang's commentary is, it suffers from certain serious defects. He was able to utilize the Mohammedan sources only in the most occasional and indirect manner. Far more serious is his neglect of the Taoist Canon, the natural place in which to seek elucidation of a Taoist text. Moreover, his commentary is not intended to be a complete annotation, but consists rather of such parallels and explanations as the writer's vast knowledge of Chinese literature immediately supplied. Points urgently requiring comment are wholly ignored ; while in other cases a passage of no particular difficulty supplies the pretext for what sometimes amounts to an independent essay rather than a " note ".

I know hardly any Russian and have therefore not been able to use the translation of Palladius, which appeared in the *Works of the Peking Mission*, Vol. IV, 1866. I have, however, had the advantage of using an English translation made from the Russian of Palladius by Gerald C. Wheeler and Semen Rapoport.

[1] *Hai-ning Wang Chung-k'o kung I-shu*, 1928. See *T'oung Pao*, 1928, p. 172.

SOURCES

CHINESE, Etc. (*a*) Secular.

I. *Mēng-ta Pei-lu*. By Chao Hung. Account of a Chinese (Sung) mission to Peking in 1221.

II. *Hei Ta Shih Luo*. By P'ēng Ta-ya and Hsü T'ing. 1237. An account of the Mongols.

III. *Shēng Wu Ch'in Chēng Lu*. Anon. 1260-1294. Campaigns of Chingiz and Ögödäi.

The above three numbers refer to the annotated texts as printed in the *Hai-ning Wang Chung-k'o kung I-shu*, Collected Works of Wang Kuo-wei (1877-1927 A.D.), published in 1928.

IV. *Hsi Yu Lu*. By Yeh-lü Ch'u-ts'ai. 1229.

See Pelliot, *T'oung Pao*, 1928, p. 172. Known to me only in quotations ; the complete work, published in Japan in 1927, I have not been able to procure.

V. *Yüan Ch'ao Pi Shih*. " Secret History of the Mongols." Edition of the *Lien-yün-i Ts'ung shu*. 1848. Compilation completed in July-August, 1240 A.D. ; this apparently refers only to the Mongol original, the date of the Chinese translation being generally assigned to 1369.

VI. *Yüan Ch'ao Pi Shih Chu*, the above with commentary by Li Wēn-t'ien. 1896.

VII. *Yüan Shih*, official history of the Mongols. 1369. Edition of the Chiang-su Shu Ch'ü, 1874.

VIII. *Hsin Yüan Shih*, the above remoulded by Ko Shao-min, *c*. 1920.

IX. *Cho Kēng Lu*, by T'ao Tsung-i. 1366. Its importance as a source is diminished by the fact that most of the information

SOURCES

which it contains exists in earlier works now accessible in the
Taoist Canon.

X. *Chingiz Khan Jitsuroku*, the Mongol text of the *Secret
History*, translated into Japanese by Naka Michiyo, 1907.

(*b*) RELIGIOUS.

XI. Taoist Canon. (Shanghai reprint, 1923 onwards.)
Works by Ch'ang-ch'un : Wieger's Nos. 134, 173, 241, 1145,
1410.
Works by Wang Chē, Nos. 1139-1142, 1216.
Works by Ma Yü, Nos. 1044, 1128, 1130, 1135, 1136.
Works by Yin Chih-p'ing. No. 1132.
Li Tao-ch'ien : *Kan-ch'üan Hsien Yüan Lu*. No. 965.
Anon : *Lung Chio Shan Chi*. No. 960.

XII. *Buddhist Tripitaka*.
(1) *Pien Wei Lu*, Nanjio, 1607. Takakusu, Vol. 52, p. 751.
Composed by Hsiang-mai in 1291.
(2) *Fo Tsu Li Tai T'ung Tsai*, Nanjio, 1637. Takakusu, Vol.
49. p. 477. Composed by Nien-ch'ang, 1323.

EUROPEAN.

XIII. W. Barthold : *Turkestan down to the Mongol
Invasion*. 1928.

XIV. Articles by Barthold in the *Encyclopaedia of Islam*.

XV. E. Bretschneider : *Medieval Researches*, 2 vols. 1886.

XVI. R. Grousset. *Histoire de l'Extrême-Orient*. 1929.

XVII. C. d'Ohsson : *Histoire des Mongols*. Amsterdam.
1852.

XVIII. E. Chavannes : *Pièces de Chancelleris Chinoises*.
(*T'oung Pao*, 1904 and 1908.)

SUN HSI'S PREFACE

THE adept Ch'ang-ch'un was certainly a true possessor of the Secret Way. By the time I reached middle age I made sure that this old man muft long ago have flown aloft and in some new guise be communing with the divinities of the clouds or conversing with the Primeval Darkness itself; and it grieved me to think that I had never met him. But in the year *chi-mao* (1219) one winter day a rumour reached me that he was living near the coaft and had juft received an invitation to make a Comfortable Journey.[1] In the spring of the following year he aftually arrived in Peking and put up in the monaftery of Jade Emptiness. I saw at my firft meeting with him—for he sat with the rigidity of a corpse, ftood with the ftiffness of a tree, moved swift as lightning and walked like a whirlwind—that he was by no means an ordinary person. Conversation with him showed me that his learning was tremendous; there seemed to be no book he had not read. Henceforward my admiration for his genius continually increased. The number of those who wished to do homage to him by formally enrolling themselves as his disciples was prodigious, and their eminence may be

[1] A journey facilitated by the Emperor.

judged by the high distinction of several important officials, now in retirement, who delighted to spend their time with him. After a while he moved to the Lung-yang temple.[1] Here he was visited by messengers bearing a second invitation, and this time he actually set out for the West. On the day of his departure, some of his Taoist followers asked him how long he should be away, and he said three years. Now the year at that time had the cyclical signs *hsin-ssŭ*, and it was the Chia-chung month (i.e. second month of 1220); and when he came back the year had the cyclical signs *chia-shēn* and it was the month Mēng-tsou (i.e. first month 1224). The accuracy with which he had predicted the duration of the journey naturally caused great astonishment. On the seventh day of that month he entered Peking and took up his residence at the Ta T'ien Ch'ang temple, having received a formal invitation.[2]

Most men nowadays, when business or public duty calls them abroad, leave their homes with reluctant feet and faces downcast at the prospect of separation. But here was the Master setting out to cover thousands of miles of most difficult country, through regions never mapped, across deserts unwatered by rain or dew, in which, though he was everywhere received with the

[1] At Tē-hsing, the modern Pao-an in Chihli.
[2] From Shih-mo Hsien-tē-pu, the Governor of Peking. See below, p. 53 (note), and p. 133.

44

utmoſt honour, it was inevitable that he should suffer considerable hardship and fatigue. Yet whenever opportunity arose he was ready to loiter on the way, enjoy the beauties of the scenery in the moſt natural and leisurely manner, write a poem, talk or laugh. To him life and death seemed a succession as inevitable as cold and heat, and neither of them occupied in his heart so much as the space of a muſtard-seed or spike of grass. Such an attitude, it will be readily admitted, is only possible for one who truly possesses the Way.

His pupil Li Chih-ch'ang was with him throughout the whole journey, and kept a record of their experiences, noting with the greateſt care the nature and degree of the difficulties—such as mountain-passes, river-crossings, bad roads and the like—with which they had to contend ; also such differences and peculiarities of climate, clothing, diet, vegetation, bird-life and inſect-life as they were able to observe. He called this record *A Journey to the Weſt*, and asked me for a preface.

So great is the world that lies within the Four Seas and so manifold are its contents that with his own ears and eyes no man can hope to know them all. Some things muſt always be left of which even the wiseſt man on earth has not direct experience. And of what lies beyond the Four Seas, this observation muſt be even truer. It is such deficiencies that a record of this kind alone can fill. I would go further and say that the use of such a work does not merely consist in supplying information to the curious ; from it may also be learned that the question of whether the Highest Man ought or ought not to take service with the temporal powers is one that can only be decided according to the circumstances of the moment.

Written on the second day of autumn in the year *mou-tzŭ* (Oct. 31, 1228) by Sun Hsi, the Recluse of the Western Brook.

THE
TRAVELS OF AN ALCHEMIST

CHAPTER I

TRANSLATION OF *Hsi Yu Chi*

MY Father and teacher, the adept Ch'ang-ch'un-tzŭ, was a member of the Ch'iu family. His name was Ch'u-chi and his literary style T'ung-mi. He was a native of Ch'i-hsia, near Tēng-chou (in the province of Shangtung). While still a young man he joined the Taoist priesthood and served the adept Chung-yang[1] at Lung-mēn, near P'an-ch'i (in the province of Shansi) for thirteen years. Here, by gradual building up of his spiritual strength and protracted study of books, he at length acquired the Way. Later[2] he returned to the coast.

Before the year *mou-yin* (1218) while the Teacher was at Tēng-chou, the Honan Government[3] several times intended to send messengers with presents for him and an invitation to visit Honan. But the plan always fell through. However, next year when he was

[1] Known in secular life as Wang Chē; died in 1170.
[2] In 1191.
[3] i.e., the Kin Tartars, who then held Central China.

47

living at Lai-chou (south-weſt of Tēng-chou) in the
Hao-t'ien temple, the Honan Moderator and the
Frontier Envoy arrived there in the fourth month and
invited him to return with them. He could not do
so, but the Envoy was able to bring back poems and
hymns written by the Maſter. Subsequently an envoy
ſtarted out from Ta-liang[1]; but on the way he heard
that Shantung had been taken by the native Chinese
dynaſty, and returned. In the eighth month the two
Chinese generals Li Ch'üan and P'ēng I-pin[2] tried to
make him go with them, but he would not. His
repeated refusals (for after this, invitations from various
places kept on pouring in) surprised the prefeᶜt of
Lai-chou. But the Maſter explained to him that his
movements were controlled by Heaven. " Such
people as you can know nothing of the matter ", he
said. " When the time comes for me to go, I shall go,
and there is no more to be said."

Not long afterwards the Mongol Emperor Chingiz
Khan sent his personal Miniſter Liu Wēn[3] with a golden
tablet in the form of a tiger's head hung about him.
On it was written the message : " This man is
empowered to aᶜt with the same freedom as I myself
should exercise, had I come in person ". With him

---

[1] In Honan. The Kin Tartars surrendered moſt of Shantung to the Southern
Sung dynaſty in 1219.
[2] For both of these, see *Sung Shih*, ch. 476.
[3] For Liu Wēn, see Introduᶜtion, p. 38.

AN ALCHEMIST

were twenty Mongols, who made known the Emperor's urgent desire that the Master should return with them. While he was hesitating, Liu Wēn said : " Your name is esteemed throughout the Four Seas, and the Emperor has sent me as his special envoy across mountains and lakes, commanding me, whether it takes months, or years, on no account to return without you ". The Master replied : " Since the war started, frontiers have continually been changing. I know that in coming you have incurred great dangers, and I am sensible of your kindness in taking this trouble on my account ". " I was acting under Imperial orders ", said Liu Wēn, " and had no choice but to exert myself to the uttermost. The Command reached me in the fifth month of the present year. I was then at the Imperial Camp in the country of the Naiman tribe.[1] In the sixth month I reached Wei-ning, to the north of Po-tēng.[2] Here I received instructions from the Wingéd-one[3] Ch'ang-chēn. In the seventh month I arrived at Tē-hsing, but as the road over the Chü-yung[4] Pass was barred, soldiers were sent from Peking to meet me. I arrived at the capital in the eighth month. The Taoists there could not tell me whether you were

[1] One of the chief Mongol tribes : subdued by Chingiz in 1206. The Camp was on the Eder, one of the sources of the Selenga. The Chinese fifth month began, in 1219, on June 14th.
[2] In Shansi.
[3] i.e., Taoist luminary. Ch'ang-chēn is another name of Li Chih-ch'ang, the author of this work.
[4] S.E. of Yen-ch'ing.

49

4

alive or not. It was only when I had passed through Chung-shan and Chēn-ting[1] that I heard you were in Lai-chou. This was finally confirmed in detail by Wu Yen and Chiang Yüan, two officials in the employ of the Protector of I-tu.[2] I wanted to send 5,000 soldiers to fetch you. But these officials said it would be imprudent to do so just at the moment when the Mongols and Kin Tartars were negotiating. A sudden incursion of troops would alarm the inhabitants of the eastern provinces, who were just beginning to settle down, and cause them to take refuge in inaccessible places or even sail away to sea. Following this advice I sent twenty men, who volunteered for the task, to ride on ahead, and when we were nearing I-tu, I sent on Wu Yen and Chiang Yüan to inform their general, Chang Lin,[3] of my arrival. Lin met me outside the walls with ten thousand men in armour. I laughed at this display, saying : ' I am on my way to visit the Adept Ch'ang-ch'un. What is the use of all these armed men ? ' Lin then dispersed his troops, and rode by my side into the town. I explained my mission thus in every town through which I passed, and nowhere encountered either nervousness or opposition. Lin even gave me post-riders, and at my next halting-place,

---

[1] In Chihli.
[2] The modern Ch'ing-chou in Shantung.
[3] The Kin general, who had surrendered his province to the (Chinese) Sung Emperor .

Wei-chou, I met your disciple Yin Chih-p'ing. In the twelfth month we reached Lai-chou and I am thus at laſt able to execute his Imperial Majeſty's Auguſt Command."

The Maſter knew that a refusal was out of the queſtion, and he said calmly to Liu Wēn : " In these parts supplies are not easy to obtain. You and your party had better go back to I-tu and wait for me there. I will join you when the ceremonies of the Shang Yüan[1] are over. You can send fifteen horse-men to fetch me. I shall be ready to ſtart on the 18th ". So Liu Wēn and his followers went back to I-tu, while the Maſter chose nineteen of his followers and with them awaited the arrival of the escort. When it came, the whole party set out along the northern side of the river Wei, as far as Ch'ing-shē (Ch'ing-chou). Here they found that Liu Wēn had already left. From General Chang Lin they learnt that on the seventh day of the firſt month[2] four hundred horsemen had appeared at Lin-tzŭ, terrifying the townsmen of Ch'ing-chou. Liu Wēn had therefore retraced his ſteps, in order to hold these marauders in check. Where Liu now was, the General could not say. The Maſter accordingly went ſtraight on through Ch'ang-shan and Tsou-p'ing, reaching

[1] The fifteenth night of the firſt month, known to Europeans by the Feaſt of Lanterns. That year it fell on February 20th.
[2] February 12th, 1220.

Chi-yang[1] at the beginning of the second month. The grandees and people of the place came out to meet him burning incense, and did homage to him at a point somewhat south of the town. The winged-ones (Taoists) led the procession, and conducted the Master with much chanting to supper in the Nurture Simplicity Cloister. Here his hosts began one and all to tell him that on the 18th day of the previous month some ten cranes had come from the north-west, crying as they sped through the clouds. They then disappeared towards the south-east. Next day, between the hours of the Dragon and the Snake (8-10 a.m.) several more cranes came from the south-west. These were followed by hundreds of others, who swooped up and down. One solitary crane, however, actually brushed the cloister with its wings and hovered near it for some time before flying away. " We now know ", said the Taoists, " that this happened at the very day and hour of your departure ", and they touched their foreheads with their hands.[2]

Here he stayed for several days. In the first decade of the second month a messenger arrived saying that Liu Wēn had quartered his troops at Chiang-ling (modern Wu-ch'iao), where a boat lay moored, awaiting the Master's arrival. Next day

---

[1] He advances along the line of the present Shantung railway, and then turns north.

[2] In sign of respectful astonishment.

he set out, and on the thirteenth day Liu Wēn
sent soldiers to meet him. The Maſter asked why
they were so late. They replied that owing to
so many of the roads being blockaded,[1] Liu Wēn
had been obliged to make an excursion to Peking, in
order to colleƈt more troops. These he had ſtationed
partly at Hsin-an, partly at Ch'ang-shan, while he
himself had put his own men into Wu-i below Shēn-
shou, in order to get the roads clear. He had been
obliged to rebuild the bridge over the Hu-t'o, and
what with this and fitting up the boat at Chiang-ling,
he had naturally got behindhand. The Maſter said
that no one but His Excellence Liu Wēn could have
managed so well. Next day they crossed the Hu-t'o
and turned northwards. On the 22nd day they
reached the Lü-kou Bridge (and crossed the Sangkan).
Outside the walls of the Capital he was met by a large
deputation of officials, commoners, Buddhiſt prieſts and
Taoiſts. He entered the city on the same day by
the Li-ts'ē Gate, the Taoiſt clergy leading the way in
ſtately procession and chanting as they went. The
Provincial Governor Shih-mo[2] ordered the Maſter to
be lodged in the Jade Emptiness temple. Henceforward the gates of the temple were besieged by

[1] Since the tranſference of the Kin capital to K'ai-fēng Fu in 1215, two rebels,
Chang Pu and Wu Hsien, had been giving great trouble, and were not yet subdued.
[2] Shih-mo Hsien-tē-pu, a Black Cathayan, appointed Darugachi of Peking by
Chingiz Khan in 1216, in succession to his father, the famous general Ming-an.

crowds that grew daily larger, some wanting verses, others begging for a name.[1] Of the foot-soldiers and horsemen who came to offer themselves as his disciples and obtained from him a Taoist name, many at once lost all desire for the disastrous career of arms; so great was his religious power. The Commissioner Wang Chi, styled Chü-ch'uan,[2] sent him a poem, and the Master replied.[3]

We now heard that the Khan had shifted his head-quarters further west. The Master feared that his great age would make him unequal to a journey involving so much fatigue and exposure, and would have preferred to interview Chingiz on his return from the western campaign. He was moreover distressed to discover that Liu Wēn proposed taking with them on the journey all the girls whom he had collected for the Khan's harem. The Master reminded him that when the men of Ch'i offered female musicians as a present to the king of Lu, Confucius quitted the State of Lu. " I ", said the Master, " am a mere mountain-savage. But I do not think you ought to expect me to travel with harem-girls." Liu Wēn was obliged to send Ho-la[4] with an urgent message to the

[1] The bestowal of a religious soubriquet.
[2] A Chinese who had taken service with the Mongols. See *Yüan Shih*, ch. 153.
[3] As indicated in the preface, most of Ch'ang-ch'un's poems are omitted in my translation.
[4] Mongol *Kara* =black. One of the four Mongol officials sent to supervise Ch'ang-ch'un's journey.

AN ALCHEMIST

Emperor. The Master also sent an appeal, asking for this arrangement to be altered. One day some one brought a picture of Lao Tzŭ crossing the Frontier,[1] by Yen Li-pēn,[2] and asked the Master to write something on it.

In the first decade of the fourth month (May 4-13) the faithful expressed the hope that he would perform the ceremonies of the Full Moon in the T'ien-ch'ang temple. He refused on the plea of his forthcoming journey. But they pleaded with him, saying that the wars were still going on. Those who survived had many of them been lucky enough to see the Master face to face and receive a share of his spiritual influence. "But the dead, wrapped in the shadow of eternal night, have not yet been laved with the blessing of your commendation,—a loss that cannot fail to embitter their lot." The Master consented.

There happened at the time to be a great drought. No sooner had the celebration of the Full Moon (May 18th) begun, than rain fell heavily. The people were afraid it would interfere with the processions. But when, soon after midday, the Master approached the altar and began to officiate, the sky suddenly cleared. The crowd was delighted and exclaimed in astonishment : " He can cause rain and stop it at his

[1] Legend says that Lao Tzŭ, the mythical founder of Taoism, ended his days among the western barbarians.
[2] Died 673.

55

will. Great indeed muft be his power in the Way, that Nature should thus obey him ! " Next day the Mafter received candidates for the priefthood in the Pao-hsüan Hall. Several cranes came flying from the north-weft and the whole assembly watched them. Prayer-slips were burnt, one of which flew up into the air and disappeared, while five cranes gambolled juft above it. The officials and grandees who were present all commented on the Mafter's extraordinary single-mindedness, which gave him so wide a control over earth and sky. An old man of Nan-t'ang (in Chihli), called Chang T'ien-tu, ftyled Tzŭ-chēn, made a *fu*[1] to celebrate this occurrence, and various gentlemen made poems.[2] When the Full Moon ceremonies were over, Liu Wēn followed the Mafter northward. Their road took them through the Chü-yung Pass, and here at night towards the far end of the Pass they met with a band of robbers. But learning who it was the fellows bowed and withdrew, saying they had no wish to difturb the Mafter. In the fifth month he reached the Lung-yang temple in Tē-hsing. Here he spent the summer, and sent a poem to the grandees and officials whom he had known in Peking. The following members of our faith exchanged poems with him daily

---

[1] A " prose-poem ".

[2] A scroll was made of these poems; Yeh-lü Ch'u-ts'ai (Works, VI, f. 13 recto) commends a certain Li Tzŭ-chin for having abftained from writing a poem and laughs at Wang Chi, whose poem appears at the beginning of the scroll.

AN ALCHEMIST

while he was lodging at the temple of Jade Emptiness :
Sun Chou, Yang Piao, Shih Hsü-ts'ai, Li Shih-ch'ien,
Liu Yung, Ch'ēn Shih-k'o, Wu Chang, Chao Chung-li,
Wang Jui, Chao Fang and Sun Hsi.[1] Wang Kou and
Wang Chēn-tsai accompanied him on his walks.

The Lung-yang monastery lies on the southern
slopes of the Ch'an-fang Mountain. The hill-side is
full of caves inhabited by Taoist ascetics, and it was
hither that the Master used to lead his friends when he
took his walks.

To the east of the temple is a large piece of flat
country, with springs that are delightfully cool and
clear. This was one of his favourite resorts, and here
he wrote the poem :

In the afternoon with face to the wind and back to the sun
   I walk,
To the far hills I stretch my eye ; they are striped with a tangle
   of cloud.
From a thousand houses, their limbs baked by the cruel
   scorching of the sun,
With one accord the people plunge in the cool, clear stream.
In this northern country, as I come and go, the world shows
   me trust ;
On the eastern mound, where I walk and play, the people
   give me room.
At the stream-side, my paddling over, I wander among the
   trees,
Loose my hair, open my shirt, and give way to Taoist dreams.

[1] Author of the foreword to this book. Most of the other persons mentioned
are known to history.

57

He celebrated the Full Moon of mid-autumn (September 13th) at home in the temple. In the afternoon he initiated his followers into the use of various spells and also received candidates for the priesthood. The huge crowd that had collected was obliged to sit all day in the open. It comprised old people and children, many of whom were severely affected by the heat. Suddenly a cloud, shaped like an umbrella, settled over the assembly and remained there for several hours, to the extreme relief and astonishment of those who sat under it. A second miracle happened in connection with the well-water, which was sufficient for a hundred people, but not for a crowd of over a thousand. The people in charge made plans beforehand for getting water from elsewhere ; but on the three days round the time of Full Moon the well brimmed with water right up to the top, and however much was drawn, remained at the same level, so great was the assistance that his virtue elicited from Heaven. At the beginning of the eighth month, in response to an invitation from his lordship Yeh-lü T'u-hua,[1] Marshal of Hsüan-tē,[2] he took up residence in the Chao-yüan temple, which lies at the north-west angle of the town. Yeh-lü, being a patron of this temple, had hastened, on receiving news of the Master's journey, to repair the

[1] A relation of Yeh-lü Ch'u-ts'ai. Biography, *Yüan Shih* 149.
[2] See p. 61.

main buildings, fill it with holy images and redecorate
all the adjoining cells and outbuildings. During the
tenth month the Memorial Hall (dedicated to the
Patriarchs and Saints) was being decorated with wall-
paintings ; but the cold weather had put a ſtop to the
work. The Maſter refused to let it be suspended,
saying : " If ever the flute of such a one as Tsou Yen[1]
could bring back the spring-time, surely you credit
me with power enough over the elements to make
this work possible ? " Presently, in the middle of
winter, the weather became as balmy as in spring ;
there were no duſt-ſtorms, and the painter was able
to finish his work.

Shortly after this A-li-hsien[2] arrived from the Tent
of Prince Tämügä ot-chigin[3] (the younger brother of
Chingiz) with an invitation to the Maſter ; he was
followed by the Commissioner Wang Chi,[4] who said
that he had received special orders from the Prince
that if the Maſter came to the Weſt he was on no
account to omit paying the Prince a visit. The
Maſter moved his head in sign of assent. This month,
when he was on an excursion to the Wang Mountains
in the north, Yeh-lü T'u-hua returned from delivering

[1] The ſtory is from Lieh Tzŭ.
[2] The "H-la-ch'ien" of the *Secret Hiſtory of the Mongols.* See Introduction,
p. 39.
[3] " The Fire Prince ", a Turkish title, given to the youngeſt son, who ſtayed at
home and minded the hearth.
[4] See above, p. 54.

his message to the Emperor. He bore a Command addressed " from the Emperor Chingiz to the Adept, Maſter Ch'iu ". This document[1] praised the Tao of the Maſter above that of the Three Philosophers (Lao Tzŭ, Lieh Tzŭ and Chuang Tzŭ) and declared that his merits were recognized in the remoteſt corners of the earth. Further on the Emperor said : " Now that your cloud-girt chariot has issued from Fairyland, the cranes that draw it will carry you pleasantly through the realms of India. Bodhidharma,[2] when he came to the Eaſt, by spiritual communication revealed the imprint on his heart ; Lao Tzŭ, when he travelled to the Weſt[3] perfeǎed his Tao by converting the Central Asians. The way before you, both by land and water, is indeed long ; but I truſt that the comforts[4] I shall provide will make it not seem long. This reply to your letter will show you my anxiety on your behalf. Having learnt that you passed safely through the severe heat of autumn, I will not now trouble you with further friendly messages ".

Such was the respeǎ with which the Emperor addressed him ! Chingiz also gave inſtruǎions to Liu Wēn that the Maſter was not to over-exert himself or go too long without food, and was to travel in comfort,

---

[1] The text is given in full at the end of the *Hsi Yu Chi.*
[2] Semi-legendary founder of the Zen Sect of Buddhism ; see above, p. 14.
[3] See above, p. 55.
[4] Lit. : " Staff and leg-reſt ", which the Book of Rites says muſt be provided for the aged, if their services are retained.

by easy stages. The Master now pointed out to Liu Wēn that in the country through which they would have to pass the weather was already becoming severe ; the passage across the Gobi was long, and the necessities of the journey still remained to be collected. Why should they not stay at the Lung-yang temple till the spring, which was the most advantageous time at which to start ? Liu Wēn accepted this proposal and on the 18th day the Master journeyed South and once more took up residence at the Lung-yang. On the fourteenth day of the eleventh month (December 10th) he attended a service at the Buddhist temple Lung-yen-ssŭ and wrote up a poem on the wall of the western gallery of the main hall.

On the 15th day of the first month (February 18th) of the next year (1221) he celebrated the Full Moon at the Chao-yüan temple in Hsüan-tē-chou.[1] Here he showed the people the following didactic verses.

A little lump of foul flesh falls to the earth
And from it shoots a demon-sprout of Good and Ill,
Fills with its leaves and laced branches the Three Worlds ;
This mighty tree whose ceaseless growth entangles Time !

The journey began on the eighth day of the second month (March 3rd) in excellent weather. His Taoist friends accompanied him to the western outskirts of the town and there standing at his horse's head they

[1] Marco Polo's Sindachu, the modern Hsüan-hua Fu.

asked him, weeping, when they might expect to see him back from this immense journey upon which he was setting out. At firſt he would say no more than that, if their hearts remained firmly set upon the Tao, they would surely see him again. But when, with tears in their eyes, they begged him to be more particular, he told them that the goings and ſtoppings of Man were determined elsewhere than on earth. " Moreover ", he said, " travelling thus into ſtrange lands I cannot yet tell whether their Tao will harmonize with mine or not ". But the people said : " Maſter, we cannot believe that you do not know these things. We beseech you to foretell them to us." He saw that there was nothing for it but to tell them, and twice he said diſtinctly, " I shall return in three years ".

On the tenth day he spent the night at Ts'ui-ping K'ou, crossing the Yeh-hu (" Wild Fox ") Range next day. Looking back southward we got a good view of the T'ai-hang and other mountains. A fresh breeze had cleared away the clouds, and the air was very agreeable. Northwards lay nothing but wintry sands and withered grass. Here China—its cuſtoms and climate—suddenly comes to an end. But muſt not the Taoiſt learn to accept gladly whatever surroundings he may find himself in ? Sung Tē-fang[1] and the reſt

[1] One of the disciples.

pointed to the skeletons lying on the battle-field[1] and said: "Let us, if we come home safely, say Masses[2] for their souls; for who knows whether our setting out on this journey was not in part fated that we might help them to Salvation?"

Going northwards we passed through Fu-chou (thirty miles from Kalgan) and travelling in a north-easterly direction we came on the 15th day (March 10th) to Kai-li-po, where the ground consists entirely of small salt-tumuli. Here we encountered the first signs of human habitation, a group of about twenty houses standing to the north of a salt-lake which winds about for a considerable distance towards the north-east. After this point there are no rivers, but frequent wells dug in the sand, from which sufficient water is procured. One may also travel due north for several thousand li[3] without coming to a single high hill. After five days on horse-back we crossed the line fortified by the Kin Tartars in the Ming-ch'ang period (1190-1196). After six or seven days we suddenly came to the great sand-desert. Like all the country from here onwards for a thousand li in a north-easterly direction it is not entirely without vegetation, for there are stunted elm-trees, the largest of which are several feet[4] in diameter. At the beginning

[1] The first important battle (1211) between the Mongols and the Kin Tartars.
[2] Lit.: "celebrate the Service of the Golden Tablets".
[3] The li of this book is about 3⅓ miles.
[4] Lit.: "an arm-hug".

of the third month we left the desert and reached
Yü-ērh-li,[1] where there is a settlement of peasants and
fishermen. The festival of Ch'ing-ming[2] was already
at hand, but here the trees showed no sign of spring,
and the ice had not begun to melt. We left this place
on the fifth day of the third month (March 30th) and
turned north-east. In the far distance on every side
we could see smoke rising from groups of black waggons
and white tents. The owners move from place to
place in search of water and pasturing-grounds. The
country is here flat, marshy, and quite unwooded.
Whichever way one looks, there is nothing to be seen
but dark clouds and pale grass. We travelled for over
twenty days in the same direction and came at last
to an arid stream that, flowing in a north-westerly
direction, ultimately joins the Kerulen River. The
water in this stream is just deep enough to touch a
horse's belly, and on its banks are numerous clumps of
willow-trees. For three days we travelled north and
came at last to a small sand-desert. On the first day
of the fourth month (April 24) we reached Prince
Tämügä's encampment. By now the ice was beginning
to melt and there was a faint touch of colour in the
grass. When we arrived a marriage was being
celebrated in the camp. From five hundred *li* round
the headmen of the tribes had come, with presents of

[1] The modern Ta-li-po.   [2] The Chinese Easter.

mares' milk, to join in the feaſt. The black waggons and felt tents ſtood in rows ; there muſt have been several thousand of them. On the seventh day the Maſter interviewed the Great Prince, who queſtioned him concerning the possibility of extending one's span of life. The Maſter said that only those who had faſted and observed certain rules could be told of these things. It was agreed that he should receive inſtruction on the day of the full moon. But by then heavy snow was falling and the matter was overlooked. Or rather, His Highness seemed to have changed his mind, for he now said that it would be improper for him to anticipate his father in receiving inſtruction from one whom the Great Khan had been at pains to summon from so great a diſtance. But he ordered A-li-hsien to bring the Maſter back to him after the interview with the Emperor was over. On the seventeenth day (May 10th) the Great Prince gave us a farewell present of several hundred oxen and horses, together with ten waggons, and we set out towards the north-weſt. On the twenty-second day (May 15th) we reached the Kerulen at the point where it swells into a lake[1] several hundred *li* in circumference. A ſtorm had caſt up some large fish of which the Mongols who were with us caught several each. Proceeding in a weſtward direction along the southern bank of the Kerulen, we

[1] Lake Hu-lun.

65

more than once came upon wild garlic, which we ate. On the firſt day of the fifth month (May 23rd) juſt at noon, there was a total eclipse[1] of the sun, during which the ſtars were visible. But the light soon returned. At the time, we were on the southern bank of the river. The eclipse worked across the sun from north-weſt to south-eaſt. In this country it is cold in the morning and hot in the evening; there are many plants with yellow flowers. The river flows to the north-eaſt. On both banks grow many tall willows. The Mongols use them to make the frame-work of their tents. After sixteen days travelling we came to a point where the Kerulen makes a loop to the north-weſt, skirting some mountains. We therefore could not follow it to its source, but turned south-weſt, into the Yü-ērh-li poſt-road. Here the Mongols we met were delighted to see the Maſter, saying they had been expeſting him since the year before. They presented him with one ſtone five pecks of barley and millet, which he reciprocated with a peck of dates. They were very pleased with his present, for they had never seen dates before. Before we parted from them they expressed their gratitude by executing a dance. We travelled on for a further ten days. At the moment of the summer solſtice the shadow (of the gnomon) according to

[1] This is expressed in an archaic phrase culled from the *Tso Chuan*. The eclipse is referred to by several other Chinese writers.

our measurement was three foot six or seven inches.[1]

The peaks of the great mountains were now gradually becoming visible. From this point onwards, as we travelled weſt, the country remained hilly and well-inhabited. The people live in black waggons and white tents ; they are all herdsmen and hunters. Their clothes are made of hides and fur ; they live on meat and curdled milk. The men wear their hair in two plaits that hang behind the ears. The married women wear a head-dress of birch-bark, some two feet high. This they generally cover with a black woollen ſtuff ; but some of the richer women use red silk. The end (of this head-dress) is like a duck ; they call it[2] *ku-ku*. They are in conſtant fear of people knocking againſt it, and are obliged to go backwards and crouching through the doorways of their tents.

They have no writing. Contraƈts are either verbal or recorded by tokens carved out of wood. Whatever food they get is shared among them, and if any one is in trouble the others haſten to his assiſtance. They are obedient to orders and unfailing in their performance

---

[1] Wylie, on the assumption that the upright objeƈt used was an 8 ft. ſtaff, tried to determine from these indications the exaƈt position of the travellers ; but uncertainty as to the charaƈter of Ch'ang-ch'un's " gnomon " makes such a calculation very hazardous. It may have been a man with upſtretched hand.

[2] i.e. the " queue ", in modern Mongol, *kükül*. For this, not the men's plaits, see A. Moſtaert, *Àpropos de quelques Portraits d' Empereurs Mongols.* Asia Major, Vol. IV, fasc. 1, p. 145. The men (see *Měng Ta Pei Lu*, f. 12 verso) shaved their heads on the crown, leaving a fan-shaped tuft over the forehead. These fashions of Mongol men and women are similarly described by Odoric, Rubruck and other travellers.

of a promise. They have indeed preserved the simplicity of primeval times.

Four stages further on, bearing north-west, we crossed a river[1] and found ourselves in a fertile plain bounded by well-wooded hills and a pretty stream. The water-plants were particularly luxuriant and fine. To east and again to west of our road we could distinguish the ruins of a deserted city. These remains were in good condition and it was possible to trace the ground-plan of the town, which did not differ from that of a Chinese city. There were no inscriptions from which we might guess the date of the place. Someone said it was built by the Kitai; and just afterwards we dug up a tile with Kitai writing on it.[2] No doubt the place was founded by that part of the Liao armies which, refusing to submit to the Kin Tartars, emigrated to the west. But the Kitai made their actual capital to the south-west, at Samarkand, the most beautiful place in the whole of the vast Muslim (Hui-ho) Empire, and seven of their emperors ruled there.[3]

[1] Probably the Karuha, an affluent of the Tola. On either bank of the Karuha Radloff's *Atlas der Altetuimer von Mongolei* marks a ruined site.

[2] This writing, made by mutilating and re-arranging Chinese characters, was concocted by order of the Kitai ruler Yeh-lü I in 920; for existing inscriptions see *T'oung Pao*, 1923, 292.

[3] The Kitai held Samarkand from 1141 to 1209, but it was never their capital. There seems here to be a confusion between Hsün-ssü-kan, the Chinese name for Samarkand and the Hu-ssŭ Ordo, the name of the encampment in the Chu valley, south of Lake Balkash, where the Kitai monarchs resided. The statement "seven emperors" is true of this capital; while during the occupation of Samarkand, there were only six emperors. It is possible, however, that Samarkand had the status of a Western Capital, though this is not recorded.

AN ALCHEMIST

On the 13th day of the sixth month (July 4th) we reached the Long Pine Range and spent the night on the other side. The country was now thickly wooded with pines and firs so lofty as to defy the clouds and hide the sun. They grow chiefly in the defiles on the northern sides of the hills, while the southern slopes are almoſt bare. On the fourteenth day we crossed another mountain and shallow river.[1] The weather was extremely cold and even the robuſter members of our party suffered severely. That night we camped on the level. Rising at dawn we found a thin coating of ice all round our tent. On the seventeenth we camped to the weſt of the ridge. Though this was the firſt of the three Seasons of Subdual[2] it froze every morning and evening, and there were three falls of hoar-froſt. The river was partly frozen and cold as in the depths of winter. The natives said that usually the snow was ſtill lying in the fifth and sixth months, and that we were lucky to have ſtruck so mild and fine a year. The Maſter altered the name of the mountains, calling them the Hugely Cold Range. Whatever rain there was tended to turn to hail. The road across the mountains kept on twiſting and turning. The direction was south-weſt[3] for a hundred *li* and then

[1] The Orkhon.
[2] The subdual of the Metal Spirit by the Fire Spirit. This firſt hot spell was supposed to begin on the " metal " day neareſt to the summer solſtice.
[3] The text says north-weſt. There is a misprint here or in the next clause.

north-weſt again. Here we came to a plain and a
ſtony river[1] that ran for some fifty *li* between banks
more than a hundred feet high. Its waters, deliciously
clear and cold, tinkle with a sound like bells of jade.

On the banks of the ravine grows a kind of leek
three or four feet high. The valley is crowned by
huge pine-trees over a hundred feet high. The
mountains to the weſt ſtretch in an unbroken line and
are all thickly covered with pine trees. We travelled
through these mountains for five or six days on a track
that wound in and out among the peaks, amid
magnificent foreſts. Below us ran a ſtream that
watered a plain covered with pines, birches and other
trees, and at times we thought we could see the smoke
of human habitations. Presently we scaled a high
ridge, arched like a rainbow, beneath which was a sheer
drop of four thousand feet, and it was terrifying to
look down at the small lake[2] below.

On the 28th day we halted to the eaſt of the Ordo,[3]
and the Mongol Commissioners went on to inform
the Empress of our arrival. Her Majeſty requeſted
the Maſter to cross the river,[4] which here flows to the
north-eaſt. It was so flooded that the water came

---

[1] The Borgartai.
[2] The Chagan Po of the maps.
[3] An *ordo* was the encampment of a chief, or more accurately, of his wives.
Chingiz's four *ordos* were under the charge of his four Empresses Börtäi, Kulan,
Yäsüi and Yäsügän respectively. But which of them was in charge of the present
ordo we do not know.
[4] The Chagan Olon of the maps.

above the axles of our cart-wheels and we were obliged
to go right through the water in order to get across.

We were soon inside the encampment ; and here
we left our waggons. On the southern bank of the
river were drawn up hundreds and thousands of
waggons and tents. Every day we received a present
of melted butter and clotted milk. Both the "Chinese"
and the Tangut princess[1] sent us warm clothing and
other comforts ; also a peck of millet and ten pounds
(*liang*) of silver. Eighty catties of flour here coſt as
much as fifty pounds (of silver), for it is brought on
the backs of camels from beyond the Yin Shan,[2] some
two thousand *li* away by foreign traders from the
Weſtern lands. It was now the period of the Second
Subdual (hot spell), but there were no flies in the
tents. Ordo is the Mongol for temporary palace, and
the palanquins, pavilions and other splendours of this
camp would certainly have aſtonished the Khans of
the ancient Huns.

On the ninth day of the seventh month (July 29th)
we set out once more, conduſted by the Commissioner
(Liu Wēn). For five or six days we travelled in a
south-weſterly direſtion. Moſt of the mountains had
snow at their peaks ; lower down were often tumuli,
and climbing to the grave-mound on the top of one

[1] The "Chinese" wife was the Kin Tartar princess who had been surrendered
to Chingiz in 1214 ; the "Tangut wife" was the daughter of the Tangut ruler
Li An-ch'üan, who was handed over to Chingiz in 1210.

[2] The T'ien Shan of modern maps.

of these were found remains of offerings to the Spirits. After two or three days we passed a mountain with a high peak as sharp as a razor-blade. This mountain is thickly covered with pines and firs, and there is a lake. We next turned southwards, passing through a large defile, and this brought us to a river that flows to the weft. Its northern banks are covered by a great variety of trees. Here, for many miles on end, wild onion grew, fragrant and in great profusion, carpeting the road-side inftead of grass. To the north are the ruins of a city called Ho-la-hsiao.[1] To the south-weft we crossed a belt of sand about 20 *li* in extent. There was hardly any water or grass. Here we saw our firft Mohammedan (Hui-ho). He was digging a canal to irrigate his barley. Five or six days later we crossed a ridge and to the south of it came upon a Mongol camp. Here we slept in a tent and at break of day again began toiling through the mountains to the south, in which we observed that there was ftill some snow. A poft-rider whom we met told us that to the north of these snowy mountains is a military colony called the " Chinkai Balagasun," or City of Chinkai,[2] also known as the place of the Granary, from the faft that there are great ftorehouses there.

On the 25th day of the 7th month (Auguft 14th)

[1] This name has been brought into relation with the modern Uliassutai. The identification is very uncertain.
[2] See Introduction, pp. 33-34.

a number of Chinese craftsmen who live there came in
a body to pay their respects to the Master, whom they
acclaimed with delight, bowing before him and leading
him on, with banners of many colours, an embroidered
baldaquin to cover him, and bouquets of sweet-
smelling flowers. There soon arrived also the two
consorts of the late Emperor Chang-tsung,[1] Lady
T'u-shan and Lady Chia-ku ; also the Lady Ch'in-
shēng, surnamed Yüan, mother of the Chinese
Princess.[2]

They met the Master with tears in their eyes, telling
him that in old days they had so many times heard
flattering accounts of his powers, that they were most
distressed to leave China without ever having seen
him. To make his acquaintance at last in such a spot
as this was indeed an unexpected pleasure !

Next day Chinkai himself came from the A-pu-han
mountains.[3] The Master said to him : " Despite my
great age, in deference to His Majesty's twice-repeated
and urgent command, I have undertaken this long
journey. Now at last, after travelling several thousand
li, I have reached the territory which you rule and to
my delight discovered that whereas in the deserts
through which I have passed, there is no sign of plough
or hoe, here the autumn harvest is already ripening.

[1] Died in 1208.
[2] i.e., of the Tangut princess, see above, p. 71.
[3] Identified with the modern Argun Mountains, S.W. of Uliassutai.

73

My own wish would be to spend the winter here, awaiting the return of the Imperial Litter. Is that not possible ? " At this point Liu Wēn interposed : " My father and mafter, you have already had the moft absolute inftructions with regard to your journey, and I muft refuse to make myself responsible for any change in your plans. The decision muft reft solely with His Excellency Chinkai ". Chinkai however said that all local governors and magiftrates had recently received inftructions that if the Adept passed through their diftrict they were on no account to detain him. This showed that the Emperor wished the interview to take place at the earlieft possible moment. " If the Mafter ftays here ", Chinkai continued, " I shall certainly be blamed. But I intend personally to accompany him on the reft of the journey and he may reft assured that I shall do everything in my power to provide for his comfort." The Mafter consented, saying that evidently his departure was ordained[1], and suggefted that omens should be taken and the day fixed. Chinkai said that it would be necessary to cut down the number of waggons and followers, and ride lightly equipped ; for ahead of them were high and difficult mountains interposed with broken and swampy ground, very unsuitable for heavy travelling. It was accordingly decided to leave behind the disciple Sung Tao-an and

---

[1] He uses a Buddhift expression ; lit. " My *karma* is like this ".

74

AN ALCHEMIST

eight others. Ground was chosen to build them a
monastery. The work was carried out entirely by
voluntary labour and contributions. Neither strength,
skill nor funds were stinted, and in less than a month
the Hall of Saints, the monks' cells, the kitchens to
the east, the cloisters to the west, and cloud-chambers[1]
on either side—were all complete, and a board set up
on which it was named the Ch'i-hsia[2] Monastery.

The crops were still standing, and at the beginning
of the eighth month frost began to fall, which obliged
the people to do their harvesting in haste. A great
wind now sprang up, blowing from the west along the
mountains to the north of us. Clouds of yellow sand
completely hid the sky and everything became so
transformed as to be unrecognizable.

On the eighth day (August 26th), taking with him
Chao Chin-ku, whose religious name was Empty Purity
and nine other disciples, and escorted by two waggons
and about twenty Mongol post-riders, the Master set
out westward along the great mountains. The
expedition was accompanied by the Commissioner Liu
Wēn and His Excellency Chinkai ; also by a hundred
mounted troops. Chinkai had a follower called Li
Chia-nu, who took occasion to tell us that once in
these mountains a spirit had cut off his back hair,

[1] This expression often merely means "monastery", "temple". But here it
seems to have its original sense of a high "cloud-topping" tower.
[2] The name of Ch'ang-ch'un's birthplace.

75

which had very much alarmed him. Chin*k*ai then told us that once not far from here the King of the Naiman Tribe had also been bewitched by a mountain spirit, the creature inducing him to part with his choicest provisions. The Master made no comment on these stories.

After travelling south-west for about three days we turned south-east and crossed a large mountain. Then passing through a deep defile, in the middle day of Autumn we came out to the north-east of the Chin Shan.[1] After a short halt we continued our journey in a southward direction. The country was now so mountainous, the ascents so formidable and the valley-gorges so precipitous and deep that the use of waggons became very difficult. The road here was first made for military purposes by the Great Khan's third son (Ögödäi).

Our cavalry escort helped us to deal with the waggons, dragging them up hill by attaching ropes to the shafts and getting them down by tying ropes to the wheels and locking them fast. We thus proceeded four stages and negotiated five successive ranges and came out at last on the south side of the mountains and halted by the side of a river.[2] Here our escorts put up a row of tents and made a regular encampment, for there was both grass and water, which made the

[1] Altai.
[2] The Ulungu.

76

place a convenient one for waiting till fresh oxen and poſt-riders caught us up.

After several days we crossed the river and going southwards passed a hill composed of many-coloured ſtones, round which there was a complete lack of vegetation. After proceeding over country of one sort and another for about 70 *li* we came to two hills of reddish colour, and 30 *li* further on, to a salt traɛt with a small sand-well in the middle of it. We halted here and prepared our food with water from the well. At the sides of the salt patch was green grass, but it was everywhere trodden down by horses and sheep. A conversation between Liu Wēn and Chin*k*ai took place, in which the former said, " This is the moſt difficult part of the journey. We will take whatever route Your Excellency advises." Chin*k*ai said that he had known this diſtriɛt for a long while (and was clear as to the course they ought to pursue). Both of them then went to lay the position before[1] the Maſter. Chin*k*ai said that they would soon arrive at the Domain of White Bones, where the ground is ſtrewn with black ſtones. Two hundred *li* further on they would come to a desert, on the northern edge of which there was abundant water and grass. They muſt then travel a hundred *li* across a desert whose extent from

---

[1] The word used implies conversation with a superior. Its other sense ("seek advice") would here be out of place.

east to west was so vast that it had never been ascertained. They would encounter no grass or water till they reached the first Mohammedan city. The Master asked why the place was called the Domain of White Bones, and Chinkai explained that it was the site of an ancient battle. An army of exhausted men had reached this place and had simply lain down and died. Less than one in a hundred had managed to reach home. More recently[1] a great Naiman army had also been defeated here. " In this desert ", said Chinkai, " the heat is so great that if the journey is made by day in fine weather both horse and rider almost invariably succumb. Starting in the evening one can get half-way across before morning, and one reaches grass and water towards noon."

We accordingly rested for a short while, and set out again at supper-time. We were obliged to cross hundreds of sand-hills and our progress was like that of a ship climbing continually over the crests of huge waves. But next day, several hours before noon, we duly reached the city of which Chinkai had spoken.

---

[1] 1208. *Cf.* the *Secret History of the Mongols*. Vol. 8. " In the Rat year (1204) Chingiz went in pursuit of (the Merkit chief) Tokto'a and having reached the Altai Mountains wintered there. In the spring of the next year (1205) he crossed the A-lai Range and found that Küchlük, chief of the Naiman and Tokto'a, chief of the Merkit had joined forces near the Ortish River. He . . . attacked them and Tokto'a was killed by a stray arrow. The enemy forces, cavalry and infantry, fled in panic across the Ortish, where more than half of them were drowned."

The *Ch'in Chēng Lu* and the Mohammedan sources are undoubtedly right in placing this event in 1208, not 1205.

AN ALCHEMIST

We had found the going by night very easy and agreeable. Our only fear was that in the pitch darkness goblins and elves might bewitch us, and to prevent this we were about to smear blood on our horses' heads, when the Mafter said to us laughing, " Do you not know that ghofts and evil spirits fly from the presence of honeft men ? There are numerous inftances of this in books which I am sure you have all read. And if this is true of ordinary people, the followers of Tao ought surely not to be afraid ". When we ftarted on our night journey our oxen were all incapable of further effort, and abandoning them by the roadside we harnessed six horses to our waggons. Henceforward we did not again use oxen. When we firft entered the desert we saw far away on the horizon to the north-weft a thin silvery flake. Our guides could not tell us what it was, but the Mafter said he was sure it was the Yin Shan (the modern T'ien-shan). Next day when crossing the desert we met some charcoal-burners and asked them. They told us that the Mafter was right.

On the 27th day of the eighth month (September 15th) we reached the foot of the Yin Shan. Here some Uighurs came out to meet us, and presently we reached a small town. The ruler of the place brought us grape-wine, choice fruits, large cakes, huge onions, and ftrips of Persian linen, a foot for each person.

They told us that three hundred *li* away, on the
other side of the Yin Shan, lay Huo-chou,[1] where
the climate was extremely hot and wine was very
plentiful. Next day we proceeded westward along
a river, passing two ¦small towns,[2] both of which were
inhabited. The corn was just ripening. The fields
are all irrigated with spring-water which is brought
by aqueducts ; for there is never enough rain to
produce a crop.

Further west is the large town of Beshbalig.[3] The
king's[4] officers, with many of the nobles and people,
and some hundred Buddhist and Taoist[5] (? Manichean)
priests came in great state a long way out of the town
to meet us. The Buddhist priests were all dressed in

---

[1] The Kao-ch'ang of Sui and T'ang times, near but not identical with the modern
Karakhōja.

[2] These, with the small town already mentioned, must be identical with the three
towns on the way to Beshbalig mentioned by the *Yüan-ho Chün Hsien Chih*—namely
Ho-chē, Yen-ch'üan and T'ē-lo. At the time of Ch'ang-ch'un's journey one of
them (as may be gathered from the Life of the Uighur Ha-la I-ha-ch'ih Pei-lu
[Kara-igach Bürlük ?]), *Yüan Shih* 124, was known as Tu-shan Ch'ēng, or "Town
of the Lonely Hill".

[3] " Five Castles." Its ruins are near the modern Kuchen.

[4] The Uighur ruler of the place, Barchuk Art Tägin, was at this time serving
Chingiz on his western campaign.

[5] There is no reason to doubt that during the Chinese occupation of Beshbalig
(middle of the seventh to middle of the eighth century) there were Taoist communities
here as in all regions where Chinese settlers penetrated. But it is improbable that
a purely Chinese sect should have survived five hundred years of Turkish, Tibetan
and Uighur occupation. That Li Chih-ch'ang should have regarded Manicheans
as analogous to Taoists is natural enough considering the enlistment of Mani into
Taoist tradition, and the dualistic basis of both religions.

As to the costume of Buddhist priests—theoretically the upper garment could be
of any drab or " broken " colour, but should not be red, white, blue, yellow or pure
black. In the paintings from Tun-huang a dull puce-grey is the favourite colour,
but a dull brown is also found.

brown. The head-dresses[1] and robes of the Taoiſts were quite different from those worn in China.

We lodged in the upper ſtory of a house looking on to a vineyard, to the weſt of the city. Here some relations of the Uighur king brought us wine as well as marvellous flowers, all kinds of fruit and choice perfumes. They also entertained us with dwarfs and musicians, all of whom were Chinese. The people of the place indeed grew daily more courteous in their attentions. Among those who came to wait upon the Maſter were Buddhiſt and Taoiſt prieſts, as well as Confucians. We asked them about the hiſtory of the place, and they said in T'ang times this was the so-called Northern Court or residence of the Chinese Governor General.

In the third year of the period Ching Lung (709) the governor was a certain Yang Kung-ho who ruled so well that the native population was devoted to him, and the effeƈts of his adminiſtration are felt even today. In the weſtern part of the Lung-hsing[2] temple are two ſtones with inscriptions in which his merits are glowingly described. The temple also contains a library of Buddhiſt books. The frontier fortifications of the T'ang dynaſty are in many places ſtill extant.

---

[1] For the tall white cylindrical hats of the Manichean Electi see von Le Coq, *Die Manichäischen Miniaturen*, Berlin, 1923. There is, however, very little other evidence that Manicheism ſtill survived at this period in Central Asia.

[2] A famous temple. It was here that Siladharma, *c.* A.D. 789, translated the *Daſabhūmi Sūtra*.

We were told that several hundred *li* to the eaſt was a city wall called Hsi-liang,[1] and three hundred *li* to the weſt a diſtrict-city called Lun-t'ai.[2]

The Maſter asked how far it ſtill was to the Khan's residence, and they all said it was about another 10,000 *li* to the south-weſt.

That night there was a ſtorm. Juſt outside our vineyard ſtood a huge tree. It was on this occasion that the Maſter composed and handed round the poem :

> At night I lodged at the foot of Yin-shan ;
> A silent night, with no sound or ſtir.
> Suddenly in the sky heavy clouds massed,
> And a tempeſt shook the leaves of the great tree.
> You speak of a voyage of ten thousand *li* ;
> Already we are come where winter knows no chill.
> Whether I live or die, what matters it now ?
> Like thiſtle-down, I will go where I am blown.

On the second day of the ninth month (September 19th) we ſtarted out again, travelling weſt for four days ; after which we camped to the eaſt of Lun-t'ai. The head of the Tarsā[3] came to meet us.

Looking south towards the Yin Shan we saw three sharp peaks ſtanding out againſt the sky. The Maſter

---

[1] The modern city of Liang-chou in Kansuh. Both direction and diſtance are only general indications.

[2] Famous in T'ang times. The ancient Lun-t'ai, of Han times, was, however south of the T'ien shan.

[3] i.e., "Quakers". This term was applied by Moslem Persians to Chriſtians and also occasionally to other non-Moslems. John of Montecorvino speaks of " Tarsic letters ", meaning the Syriac script used by Neſtorian Chriſtians.

made a poem about them and presented it to the
student Li Po-hsiang (this student is a phrenologist).
After passing through two other towns we reached
Chambalig.[1] The ruler is an Uighur and an old friend
of Chinkai. He brought with him all his family and
a number of Hui-ho priests, who came a long way out
to meet us. Upon our arrival we were entertained
upon a terrace and the Uighur ruler's wife gave us
grape-wine, and also put in front of us water-melons
that weighed as much as a measure[2] each, and sweet
melons as large as (porcelain) pillows. Their scent
and taste is quite different from what we are used to
in China ; but the garden-vegetables are the same as
ours. A priest came and waited upon the Master.
By means of an interpreter he asked this priest what
scriptures he read. He replied that since he had
received the tonsure and submitted to the rules of
the order, he had worshipped the Buddha and followed
no other teaching ; which was natural enough, for the
dominions of the T'ang dynasty extended to this place.
But west of this one finds no Buddhist priests,[3] the
Hui-ho people only worshipping the western quarter.[4]
Next day we proceeded westwards along the Yin

---

[1] According to the *T'ang Shu*, 150 *li* west of Lun-t'ai is the moated city of Chang
(Chang being a common Chinese surname). Chambalig, therefore, may mean
" the City of Chang ".
[2] About 30 pounds.
[3] " Or Taoists ", adds the text printed in the *Lien Yün-i Ts'ung Shu*.
[4] i.e., praying towards Mecca.

Shan for about ten ſtages ; then we crossed a sand-belt, composed of such fine sand that the wind worked upon it exactly as upon water, gathering it into masses that piled up and then suddenly dispersed like waves on a ſtormy sea. There was a complete lack of vegetation ; our horses and carts progressed with great difficulty, and it was only after ſtruggling for a whole day and night that we at laſt got across. This appears to be an arm of the White Bones desert mentioned above.[1] On the south it goes right up to the foot of the Yin Shan. For five more days we travelled over sandy ground and finally camped on the northern slopes of the Yin Shan.

Next day, ſtarting early in the morning, we travelled southward for about seventy or eighty *li*, down hill all the way, and halted at dusk. The cold was intense, and there was no water. Rising at dawn we proceeded south-weſt for about twenty *li* and came suddenly upon a large lake,[2] about two hundred *li* in circumference, surrounded by snow-capped peaks, that were reflected in its waters. The Maſter called it the Heavenly Lake. We followed the shores of the lake due south and descended a deep ravine,[3] the precipitous sides of which were covered from top to foot with an incredible profusion of pines and birch-trees. Stream

[1] See above, p. 77.
[2] The Sairam.
[3] The Pine-tree Pass, " Sung Shu T'ou ".

AN ALCHEMIST

after ſtream rushes down into this defile, forming a torrent that bends and twiſts down the pass for a diſtance of sixty or seventy[1] *li*. It was the Great Khan's second son (Chagaṭai), who when accompanying his father on the weſtern campaign firſt conſtructed a road through the defile, piercing the rocks of and building no less than forty-eight timber bridges of such width that two carts can drive over them side by side.

When the light began to fail we camped in the ravine and next morning came out into a large valley running eaſt and weſt. A river runs through it and everywhere there was abundance of water and paſture. There was a feeling of spring in the air, and here and there a few mulberry and jujube-trees.

One more ſtage brought us to the town of Almalig,[2] which we reached on the 27th day of the ninth month. We were met by the Moslem[3] ruler of the place and the Mongol darugachi (governor) with their retinues. They gave us lodging in a fruit-garden to the weſt. The natives call fruit *a-li-ma*, and it is from the

[1] The " six or seven " of some texts is probably a misprint.
[2] North-weſt of the modern Kulja. " Alma " means " apple " in the Turkic languages.
[3] Moslem is written " P'u-su-man ". His name (to give it its Arabic form) was Sugnāq-tagīn. He was the son of a highwayman called Būzār. Later he married the Great Khan's grand-daughter Bulgan-Bigä. The identification of this personage was firſt made by Hung Chün (died, 1893) in his unpublished commentary on the *Hsi Yu Chi*, on the ſtrength of a passage in d'Ohsson's *Hiſtoire des Mongols*. M. Pelliot (*T'oung Pao*, 1928, 174) says that Hung's commentary is probably loſt; but Wang Kuo-wei's note on the present passage shows that he was able to consult Hung's commentary in 1925-6, so that it presumably ſtill exiſts.

85

abundance of its fruits that the town derives its name. It is here that they make the stuff called " tu-lu-ma "[1] which gave rise to the popular story about a material made from " sheep's wool planted in the ground ".[1] We now procured seven pieces of it to make into winter clothes. In appearance and texture it is like Chinese willow-down—very fine, soft and clean. Out of it they make thread, ropes, cloth and wadding.

The farmers irrigate their fields with canals ; but the only method employed by the people of these parts for drawing water is to dip a pitcher and carry it on the head. Our Chinese buckets delighted them. " You T'ao-hua-shih[2] are so clever at everything ! ", they said. T'ao-hua-shih is their name for the Chinese. Every day the people brought us an increasing number of presents.

Our journey began again with four days travel to the west. This brought us to the Ta-la-su[3] Mu-nien. " Mu-nien " means river.[4]

[1] The Chinese, being unfamiliar with cotton, could not believe that a stuff was obtained by cultivating a tree, and imagined that a lamb, being buried, produced a crop of fresh lambs next year. This legend can be traced back in China to the sixth century. Allusions to it are frequent in Chinese literature.

[2] Representing Tavkash or the like. This designation of the Chinese occurs in the early Turkic inscriptions on the Orkhon in the form Tabkach. The same word occurs in Byzantine Greek in the form Ταυγαστ. The popular etymology, which sees in it a corruption of " T'ang Chia Tzŭ ", " Children of the House of T'ang ", is not rendered more convincing by the arguments of Dr. Kuwabara, *Memoirs* . . . *of the Tōyō Bunko*, No. 1, pp. 73-78. For the Uighur form Tvgach, see F. W. K. Müller, *Uigburica*, I, 1908, p. 13.

[3] Talas. The Ili River is meant. The modern Talas River is a long way further west.

[4] Mongol, *Mürän*.

AN ALCHEMIST

It is deep and broad, and flows towards the north-west. In its passage from the east it cuts right through the Yin Shan. South of the river are more snow-mountains. On the second day of the tenth month (October 18th) we crossed it in a boat, and going southwards came to a large mountain with a small town on its northern slopes. When we had proceeded westwards for five days more, as the journey which the Master had undertaken at His Majesty's command was now drawing to a close and we were near the temporary Residence, the envoy Liu Wēn went on ahead to announce our approach, leaving us in charge of Lord Chinkai. We had travelled for seven days more and were crossing a range to the south-west when we met an ambassador of the Eastern Hsia kingdom[1], who was on his way back to China. He came and did reverence before the Master's tent. We asked him how long it was since he left the Khan's headquarters. He said he had started on the 12th day of the seventh month (August 1st), and that Chingiz with his army was at present pursuing the Sultan Khan[2] into India.

Next day it snowed heavily. We came to a small

---

[1] This kingdom was founded in Manchuria in 1216 by a certain Fu-hsien Wan-nu (a Kin Tartar). The same person had already founded a kingdom once before, and been suppressed by Chingiz. Three years later (in 1224) he tried once more to become independent. But in a poem written before the death of Chingiz (1227) Yeh-lü Ch'u-ts'ai speaks of the Eastern Hsia kingdom as already defunct.

[2] The Khwārizm-shah, Jalāl-al-Dīn. This event, which is here correctly placed in 1221, is put a year later by the *Shēng Wu Ch'in Chēng Lu* and the *Yüan Shih*, as also by Rashid-ed-Dīn. The mistake is part of a general error in chronology by which in these three works the events of 1220-1224 are all placed a year too late.

Hui-ho town where the snow lay a foot deep. But when the sun came out, it melted. On the sixteenth day (November 1st) going south-west we crossed a wooden bridge[1] and in the evening came to the foot of the Nan Shan. Here was the capital[2] of Ta-shih Lin-ya. The rulers of this kingdom were descendants of the Liao (Kitai) dynasty. When the Kin Tartars overthrew the Liao,[3] Ta-shih at the head of several thousand men retreated to the north-west. It was only after wandering for about ten years that he at last came to this place. The climate and weather are here quite different from what one finds north of the Chin Shan (Altai). There is much flat land, in which mulberry-trees are grown,[4] crops reared and wine, too, is made from grapes. The fruits are the same as in China ; but as no rain falls during the summer or autumn, they are obliged to irrigate their fields by digging channels from the rivers. In this way they get quite good harvests. To the north-east and north-west there are mountains and ravines on every side, stretching without a break for ten thousand *li*.

It is said that Ta-shih's empire lasted about a hundred years.[5] When the Naiman tribe was defeated[6] they

[1] The Chu River.
[2] Balāsāgūn, where Yeh-lū Ta-shih made his capital, *c.* 1134. " Lin-ya " is a title, meaning Academician. See Introduction, p. 2.
[3] In 1124-5.
[4] For breeding silk-worms.
[5] *c.* 1124-*c.* 1211.
[6] 1206-8, by Chingiz Khan.

AN ALCHEMIST

took refuge with the Ta-shih (i.e. with the *Kara-kitai*) ; but having recuperated their ftrength they presently seized the land that had sheltered them,[1] while the weftern part of the empire was shorn off and allotted to the Khwārizm Shāh. Finally when the Heavenly Troops[2] appeared, both the Naiman and the Shah were crushed.

We now heard that the road in front of us was very difficult going. One of our wagons had broken down, and we were obliged to leave it behind. On the eighteenth day (November 3rd) we began to follow the course of the mountains in a weftward direction, and and so continued for seven or eight days. The mountain chain then suddenly bent towards the south and we came to a city[3] built of some very red kind of ftone. There are traces of an old military encampment, and to the weft, a number of great mounds, set like the ftars in the Polar Conftellation. We then crossed the river by a ftone bridge and went on through the hills to the south-weft for five ftages, finally reaching the town of Sairam,[4] where there is a small pagoda. The local ruler met us and brought us to the gueft-house of his residence.

[1] Cheluku, the laft emperor of the *Kara-kitai*, gave the Naiman prince Kûchlûk his daughter in marriage. In 1210 Kûchlûk conspired with Muhammed to overthrow his benefactor. See Introduction, p. 3.
[2] i.e., the armies of Chingiz Khan, in 1218.
[3] Talas, near the modern Aulie-ata.
[4] The Nu-ch'ih-Chien (Nudjkand ?) of the Buddhift pilgrim Hsüan-tsang.

At the beginning of the eleventh month heavy rain fell continuously for several days. On the fourth day the people of the place keep their New Year,[1] and were all greeting one another with good wishes. On the same day the reverend Hsü-ching (in secular life, Chao Chin-ku) said to Yin Chih-p'ing : " When I was in Hsüan-tē with the Master, I had a presentiment that I was fated never to return. I am worn out by the journey ; but I have not forgotten how our Master told us that to Men of Tao life and death should be indifferent, pleasure and pain should have no hold upon us. What comes, must be faced. For me it is time to depart. I hope the rest of you will serve our Father and Master with all your might ". A few days afterwards he fell sick and died. This was on the fifth day of the eleventh month (November 20th). The Master told us to bury him in the plain to the east of the town. We then proceeded south-west and after three days reached a town.[2] Here too the ruler was a Hui-ho. He was a very old man. He sent to meet us, gave us presents and an offering of hot cakes. Next day we passed through another town.[3] Two days later we came to a river called the Khojand Mürän,[4] which we crossed by a floating bridge, and halted on the

[1] Not the New Year, but the Little Festival after the close of Ramadān ; November 17th-19th, in the year 1221.
[2] Tashkent.
[3] The " Bānākit " of Rashid-ed-din.
[4] The Syr Darya.

western bank. The bridge-keeper brought to his lordship Chin*k*ai a huge fish with no scales.[1] This river has its source between two large snow-mountains to the south-east. Its waters are muddy, but swift. It is forty or fifty feet deep, and ſtretches away to the north-weſt for no one knows how many thousand *li*. South-weſt of this river there is no water or grass for about two hundred *li*, so we travelled only by night. To the south we saw great snow-capped mountains, and turned to the weſt. These mountains conneçt with those to the south of Samarkand.

Presently we came to a town[2] where there was grass and water and soon through another town where the Hui-ho chief came out a long way to meet us. We were given dinner to the south of the town and offered grape-wine. Small boys were also made to entertain us with tight-rope walking and sword-dancing. After this we passed through two more towns, and then travelled through the mountains for half a day and came out into a valley[3] running from south to north. Here we spent the night under a huge mulberry-tree which could have sheltered a hundred people. Soon we came to a town, and at the side of the road saw a well more than a hundred feet

[1] A sheat-fish.
[2] The modern Uratube, the Tung Ts'ao of ancient times.
[3] The Zarafshān.

deep. An old native of these parts was driving a bullock that turned a windlass to draw water for any one who needed a drink. This man was noticed by the Great Khan when he was on his way to conquer the West. He was much struck, and gave orders that the old man should in future be exempt from taxes and corvée.

On the eighteenth day of the eleventh month (December 3rd, 1221) after crossing a great river, we reached the northern outskirts of the mighty city of Samarkand. The Civil Governor his Highness I-la,[1] together with the Mongol and local authorities, came to meet us outside the town. They brought wine and set up a great number of tents. Here we brought our wagons to a stop. The envoy Liu Wēn, who had not been able to get far owing to the road being blocked, now said to the Master when seated with him : " I have just learnt that it is at present impossible to cross the great river[2] which lies a thousand *li* ahead of us, as native bandits have destroyed the boats and bridge. Moreover it is now the middle of winter. Would it not be better, my father and master, if your meeting with the Great Khan took place in the spring ? " The Master agreed.

After a time we entered the city by the north-east gate. The town is built along canals. As no rain

[1] Yeh-lü (I-la) A-hai.   [2] The Amu Darya.

falls during the summer and autumn, two rivers have been diverted so as to run along every street, thus giving a supply of water to all the inhabitants. Before the defeat of the Khwārizm Shah there was a fixed population here of more than 100,000 households ; but now there is only about a quarter this number, of whom a very large proportion are native Hui-ho. But these people are quite unable to manage their fields and orchards for themselves, and are obliged to call in Chinese, Kitai and Tanguts. The administration of the town is also conducted by people of very various nationality. Chinese craftsmen are found everywhere. Within the city is a mound about a hundred feet high on which stands the Khwārizm Shah's new palace. The Mongol Governor at first resided here. But the local population was exasperated by famine and there was perpetual brigandage. Fearing trouble, the Governor went to live on the north side of the river. The Master however, consented to live in this palace, saying with a sigh : " The Man of Tao lets fate lead him whither it will and measure his days as it may choose. Even when a naked sword is at his throat, he does not blench. How then should he be in panic at a rising that has not even taken place ? Moreover Good and Evil go their own way, without harming one another ". His followers were thus re-assured.

The Governor gave a banquet in his honour, and

93

sent ten pieces of gold brocade, but the Master would not receive them. After that he sent a monthly allowance of rice, corn-flour, salt, oil, fruits, vegetables and so on ; he became every day more attentive and respectful. Noticing that the Master drank very little he begged to be allowed to press a hundred pounds of grapes and make him some new wine. But the Master answered : " I do not need wine. But let me have the hundred pounds of grapes ; they will enable me to entertain my visitors ".

These grapes keep for a whole winter. We also saw peacocks and large elephants[1] which come from India, several thousand *li* to the south-east.

While the Master was passing the winter at Samarkand, Liu Wēn and the Chancellor Chinkai gave him Ho-la[2] to attend upon him. Meanwhile Liu Wēn at the head of several hundred armed men went ahead to inspect the roads.

A number of Chinese came to pay their respects, and they once had an astronomer with them. He asked this astronomer about the eclipse on the first day of the fifth month. The man said : " Here the eclipse was at its full at the hour of the Dragon, when it covered three-fifths of the sun ".

[1] " Il y avait dans Samarkand vingt éléphants de guerre qui appartenaient au Sultan," d'Ohsson, *Histoire des Mongols*, I, 240.

[2] One of the two Mongol tribesmen mentioned at the end of the book. The other was Pa-hai.

AN ALCHEMIST

"We were by the Kerulen River", said the Master; "the eclipse was total towards mid-day. But when we came south-west to the Chin Shan, the people there said that at the hour of the Snake it reached its greatest extent, covering seven-tenths. Thus in three places it was seen in three different ways. K'ung Ying-ta (574-648 A.D.), in his commentary on the *Springs and Autumns* says that when the moon comes between us and the sun, there is an eclipse of the sun. In the present case only those who were in a direct line with the sun and moon, experienced a total eclipse. By those away from this line the eclipse is seen differently, the gradual change becoming considerable at a distance of a thousand *li*. It is just as though one covered a candle with a fan. In the direct shadow of the fan there is no light, but the further one moves to the side, the greater the light becomes."

The Master went one day to the Old Palace and wrote upon the walls two *tz'u*[1] in the metre "The Phœnix Lodges in the Wu-tree".

At the end of the intercalary[2] month (February 12th, 1222) the envoy and his horsemen returned from their reconnoitring. Liu Wēn reported to the Master that the Khan's second son (Chagatai) had advanced with

---

[1] Poems written to song-tunes, in lines of uneven length.
[2] The Chinese use an occasional thirteenth month in order to adjust their calendar.

95

his troops and repaired the damaged boats and bridges. The local bandits were dispersed, Ho-la, Pa-hai and others had been to the Prince's camp and informed him that the Master desired an audience with the Emperor. The prince replied that his father had proceeded to the south-east of the Great Snow Mountains (Hindukush), but that the snow in the mountain pass at present lay very deep for more than a hundred *li*, and it would be impossible to get through. The prince, however, pointed out that his own encampment lay directly on the route to the Emperor's, and invited the Master to stay with him, till a journey across the mountains was practicable. He promised the Master that a Mongol escort should fetch him from the city and afford him every protection on the way.

The Master, however, did not take kindly to this idea and said that he had heard for a thousand *li* to the south of the river (the Amu Darya) there is no vegetable food at all. " My diet ", said he, " consists of rice, meal and vegetables. Please convey this fact to the Khan's son."

In the first month of the new year (February 13th-March 15th, 1222) the almond trees began to bloom. They are like small peach-trees. In the autumn the fruit is picked and eaten. It tastes like walnuts. On the second day of the second month, at the spring

96

equinox, the flowers were already falling from the apricot trees.

Li, who was in charge of the Observatory, and others, asked the Master to go for a walk to the west of the town. The envoy and other officials came, bringing us grape-wine. That day there was not a cloud, and the air was very clear. Wherever we went we came to terraces, lakes, pagodas and towers, with here and there an orchard or vegetable garden. We lay and rested on the grass, all of us very happy. The mysteries of Tao were discussed and from time to time wine was handed round. The sun was already setting when we returned.

The fifteenth of the second month (March 29th) was the hundred and fifth day (after the winter solstice, December 14th), and on the same day is celebrated the festival of the Great High Pure Original One.[1] The officials again invited the Master to take a walk to the west of the town. Woods and gardens stretched continuously for over a hundred *li*. There are none in China to surpass them. But here the woods are silent, for there are no song-birds.

In the first ten days of the month, A-li-hsien arrived from the Emperor's encampment with the following message : " Adept ! You have spared yourself no

<hr/>

[1] The birthday of Lao Tzŭ, the founder of Taoism. The "hundred and fifth day " is the festival of Han Shih (" Cold Eating "), the Chinese Lent. It happened in this year to fall on Lao Tzŭ's birthday.

pains in coming to me across hill and ſtream, all the way from the lands of sunrise. Now I am on my way home and am impatient to hear your teaching. I hope you are not too tired to come and meet me ". For the envoy Liu Wēn there was a further message : " I count on you to convey my message and persuade him to come. If you are successful in this, I shall not fail one day to reward you with rich lands ". Finally he sent to Chin*k*ai the message : " By your careful supervision of the Adept's journey, you have earned my gratitude ". The Commander-in-chief Bo'orju[1] was ordered to convey him through the Iron Gate Pass with an escort of a thousand armed men. The Maſter asked A-li-hsien about the route which they were about to follow, and he replied : " I myself left here on the thirteenth day of the firſt month (February 25th), and after travelling for three days towards the south-eaſt I went through the Iron Gates. Then after five days I crossed a large river.[2] On the firſt of the second month (March 15th), travelling towards the south-eaſt, I crossed the Great Snow Mountains. The snow was so deep that when I plunged my riding-whip into it, I did not get near the bottom. Even the trodden snow of the roadway was about five foot deep. We then went south for three days, and arrived at the

---

[1] One of the three chief commanders of the Mongol army.
[2] The Amu Darya.

AN ALCHEMIST

Khan's camp.[1] I gave an account of your arrival, at the news of which he was delighted. I was there several days, and then came back to Samarkand ". The Maſter left Yin Chih-p'ing and two other disciples in his quarters and taking with him five or six disciples, together with Liu Wēn and the reſt, he set out on the fifteenth day of the third month (April 28th), and on the fourth day passed through the town of Chieh-shih (Kesh),[2] where the commander Bo'orju, having already received the Emperor's inſtructions, was waiting with a thousand Mongol and native troops to escort the Maſter through the Iron Gates (the modern Buzgala Defile, 55 miles south of Kesh). Proceeding in a south-eaſterly direction we crossed some very high mountains. The way was ſtrewn with boulders and it took the ſtrength of our whole escort to get our wagons along. We were two days crossing this pass. We then came out into a valley, and followed the ſtream southwards. Our convoy was obliged to turn back northwards into the mountains, to deal with some brigands. On the fifth day we reached a small river which we crossed in boats. The banks were thickly

[1] This lay, apparently, south of the Hindukush and north of Kabul. Wang Kuo-wei identifies the place with the T'a-li-han of the *Shēng Wu Lu* (f. 62 verso), where Chingiz spent the hot season of 1221, and at the same time with the Taican of Marco Polo (Yule, I, 153). But Polo's Taican was on the road from Balkh to Badakshan, while the place in the hills of which the Khan spent the summer of 1221 was the other Talkhan, in Khurasan, on the road from Balkh to Merv. Both places are north of the Hindukush, and can have nothing to do with the site of Chingiz's camp in the spring of 1222.

[2] The modern Shahr-i-sabz.

wooded. On the seventh day we crossed a large river called the A-mu Mu-nien (Amu Darya).

Hence we travelled south-east, and towards evening halted near an ancient canal. On its banks grew reeds of a peculiar kind not found in China. The larger ones keep green all through the winter. Some of these we took and made into walking-sticks. Some we used that night to hold up the wagon-shafts, and so strong were they that they did not break. On the small reeds the leaves fall off in winter and grow afresh in the spring. A little to the south, in the hills, there is a large bamboo with pith inside. This is used by the soldiers to make lances and spears. We also saw lizards about three feet long, blue-black in colour.

It was now the twenty-ninth of the third month (May 11th) and the Master made a poem.[1] After four more days of travelling we reached the Khan's camp. He sent his high officer, Ho-la-po-tē[2] to meet us. This was on the fifth day of the fourth month. When arrangements had been made for the Master's lodging, he at once presented himself to the Emperor, who expressed his gratitude, saying : " Other rulers summoned you, but you would not go to them. And now you have come ten thousand *li* to see me. I take this as a high compliment ".

[1] As was customary at the end of spring.
[2] Not identified ; possibly represents the Mongol name *K*ara-ba'adur.

AN ALCHEMIST

The Master replied : " That I, a hermit of the mountains, should come at your Majesty's bidding was the will of Heaven ". Chingiz was delighted, begged him to be seated and ordered food to be served. Then he asked him : " Adept, what Medicine of Long Life have you brought me from afar ? " The Master replied : " I have means of protecting life, but no elixir that will prolong it ". The Emperor was pleased with his candour, and had two tents for the Master and his disciples set up to the east of his own. The interpreter now said to him : " People call you ' Tängri Möngkä Kün '.[1] Did you choose this name yourself or did others give it to you ? " He answered : " I, the hermit of the mountains, did not give myself this name. Others gave it to me". The interpreter subsequently came to him on the Emperor's behalf and asked another question. " What ", he said, " were you called in former days ? " He replied that he had been one of four pupils who studied under Chung-yang. The other three had all grown wings, and only he was left in the world. " People ", he said, " generally call me *hsien-shēng* (' senior ')." The Emperor asked Chinkai what he ought to call the Adept. " Well, some people ", said Chinkai, " call him ' Father and

---

[1] Mongol, " The Heavenly Eternal Man ". *Kün*, the Mongol for " man " is derived from an original *kümün*. It appears in the *Secret History* as *gü'ün*. A note in the text says the title means *t'ien-jēn* (heavenly man). More probably *tängri* stands for *shēn* (divine) and *möngkä kün* for *hsien* (immortal).

THE TRAVELS OF

Maſter'; others, 'The Adept'; others, the holy
hsien."[1] "From now onwards", said the Emperor,
"he shall be called the holy *hsien*."

The weather was becoming very hot and the
Emperor now moved to a high point[2] on the Snow
Mountains to escape the heat, and the Maſter accompanied him. The Emperor appointed the fourteenth
of the fourth month (June 24th) as the day on which he
would queſtion the Maſter about the Way. This
engagement was recorded by his ſtate officers, Chinkai,
Liu Wēn and A-li-hsien, as well as by three of his
personal attendants. But juſt as the time was
arriving, news came that the native mountain bandits
were in insurrection. The Emperor was determined
to deal with them himself, and put off the meeting
till the firſt of the tenth[3] month (November 5th). The
Maſter begged that he might be allowed to return to
his former quarters in the city. "Then", said the
Khan, "you will have the fatigue of travelling all the
way back here again." The Maſter said it was only a
matter of twenty days journey, and when the Khan
objeēted that he had no one whom he could give him
as an escort the Maſter suggeſted the envoy Yang
A-kou. Accordingly three days later the Khan

[1] A *hsien* is an etherealized mortal, who eventually flies away to heaven either
in the form of a bird or riding on a bird's back.
[2] Called, by the *Shēng Wu Ch'in Chēng Lu* "Pa-lu-wan Valley" and by the
Secret Hiſtory "Pa-lu-an"; the modern Perwān in Afghaniſtan, north of Kabul.
[3] "Tenth" is possibly a misprint for "seventh"; see below.

AN ALCHEMIST

ordered Yang A-kou to take with him one of the native chieftains and about a thousand horsemen, with whom he was to escort the Master back (to Samarkand) by a different way.

We crossed a great mountain where there is a " stone gate ", the pillars of which look like tapering candles. Lying across them at the top is a huge slab of rock, which forms a sort of bridge. The stream below is very swift, and our horsemen in goading the pack-asses across lost many of them by drowning. On the banks of the stream were the carcases of other animals that had perished in the same way. The place is a frontier pass, which the troops had quite recently stormed. When we got out of the defile, the Master wrote two poems.

Now when he reached the Khan's camp, at the end of the third month the grass was green and trees everywhere in bloom, and the sheep and horses were well grown. But when with the Khan's permission he left, at the end[1] of the fourth month, there was no longer a blade of grass or any vegetation. On this subject the Master wrote a set of verses.

On the road we met people coming back from the West, carrying a lot of coral. Some of the officers in our escort bought fifty branches for two bars of silver.

[1] It must actually have been about the middle of the fourth month (May 27th) that he left.

The largest was over a foot long. But as they were on horseback it was impossible to prevent it getting broken. We now continually travelled by night, to take advantage of the cool, and thus after five or six days we got back to Samarkand. All the officials of the place came to welcome the Master in his rooms. It was the fifth of the fifth month (June 15th).

Chapter II

THE envoy Li was going to China, and the Master gave him a poem addressed to the Taoist community in the east. The Master was now back in his old quarters, which stood on the northern heights some hundred feet above a clear stream, the waters of which come from the Snow Mountains and are therefore very cold. In the fifth month, when the hot season began, he would lie in a verandah at the back of the house, with the wind blowing on him. At night he slept on a terrace at the top of the building. In the sixth month, when the hot season is at its height, he bathed in the lake ; and thus, although he was so far from home, his existence was by no means disagreeable.

The arable land in the district is suitable for the cultivation of most kinds of corn ; but buckwheat and the soya-bean are not grown. Wheat ripens in the fourth month. The people here have their own way of harvesting it : they simply stack it in heaps and fetch a little to grind as they require it. By the sixth month the crops are all cut. Mr. Li, the intendant of the Governor (Yeh-lü A-hai) presented us with five acres of melon-field. The melons are extraordinarily sweet and fragrant ; there are none quite like them in China. Some of them are as large as a peck-measure.

In the sixth month the second prince (Chagatai) came back to Samarkand and Liu Wēn begged from us some of these melons to give as a present to the prince. Ten of them weighed a full hod.[1] Fruit and vegetables are very abundant ; the only sort lacking are the colocasia and cheſtnut. The aubergines are like huge coarse fingers, purple-black in colour.

Both men and women plait their hair. The men's hats are often like *yüan-shan-mao*,[2] trimmed with all kinds of coloured ſtuffs, which are embroidered with cloud-patterns, and from the hats hang tasseled pendants. They are worn by all holders of official rank, from the notables downwards. The common people merely wear round their heads a piece of white muslin about six feet long. The wives of rich or important people wind round their heads a piece of black or purple gauze some six or seven feet long. This sometimes has flowers embroidered on it or woven patterns. The hair is always worn hanging down. Some cover it in a bag of floss-silk which may be either plain or coloured ; others wear a bag of cloth or plain silk. Those who cover their heads with cotton or silk look juſt like Buddhiſt nuns. It is the women of the

---

[1] Over fifty pounds ?
[2] " Diſtant-mountain-caps " ; worn in theatrical performances ?

AN ALCHEMIST

common people who do so. Their clothes are generally made of cotton, sewn like a ſtraining-bag, narrow at the top and wide at the bottom, with sleeves sewn on. This is called the under robe and is worn by men and women alike. Their carriages, boats and agricultural implements are made very differently from ours. Their vessels are usually of brass or copper ; sometimes of porcelain. They have a kind of porcelain that is very like our Ting[1] ware. For holding wire they use only glass. Their weapons are made of ſteel. In their markets they use gold coins without a hole in the middle.[2] There are native written charaＣters on both sides. The people are often very tall and ſtrong ; so much so that they can carry the heavieſt load without a carrying-beam. If a woman marries and the husband becomes poor, she may go to another husband. If he goes on a journey and does not come back for three months, his wife is allowed to marry again. Oddly enough some of the women have beards and mouſtaches. There are certain persons called *dashman*[3] who underſtand the writing of the country and are in charge of records and documents.

At the end of the winter they have a great faſt[4] that goes on for a month. Every evening the head

[1] A very delicate kind of porcelain, usually white.
[2] " These eyeless coins how am I to ſtring ? " says Yeh-lü Ch'u-ts'ai in a poem.
[3] Mongol form of the Persian *dānishmand*.
[4] The faſt of Ramadän, which is of course variable. It began on October 9th in 1222.

of the family himself slays a sheep and divides it among those present, the meal going on continuously until next morning. In the remaining months there are six other fasts. Again, from the top of a high building they project great logs of wood like flying eave-beams (that make a platform) some ten foot square, and on it they construct a small bare chamber hung round with tasseled pendants.[1] Every morning and evening the leading man goes up there and bows to the west. This is called " addressing Heaven ". They do not pray either to Buddha or to the Taoist divinities. He sings up there in a long drawn-out chant and when they hear his voice all able-bodied men and women must at once run thither and bow down. This happens all over the country. Any one who disobeys is slain and his body cast into the market-place. The leader's clothes do not differ from those of his countrymen, save that his head is bound with a scarf of fine muslin thirty-two feet long, supported on a frame-work of bamboo.

In the seventh month, on the night of the new moon's first appearance, the Master sent A-li-hsien to remind the Khan that the time fixed for the Master's exposition of the Way had now arrived. A reply admitting this came on the seventh day of the eighth

---

[1] For minarets with wooden galleries in Persia, see *Encyclopædia of Islam*, under " Manava ". I am told that they are still to be found in Bosnia.

month (September 13th), and we set out immediately. The Governor (Yeh-lü A-hai) accompanied us for several tens of *li.* The Master said to him : " To the east of the native[1] city two thousand households have lately broken into revolt. Every night the city is lit up with flames and there is great anxiety among the people. I would rather you went back and calmed them ". " But if by any unlikely chance something should happen to you on the road ", said the Governor, " what then ? " " That ", said the Master, " is none of your business ", and persuaded him to return.

On the twelfth we passed through Kesh and on the following day were joined by an escort of a thousand men on foot and three hundred horsemen. We entered the great mountains by a different road, which avoids the Iron Gates. We crossed a stream with red waters. It runs through a gorge with cliffs several *li* high. Following the stream south-eastwards we came to a salt-spring at the foot of a mountain. In the sun its brackish waters evaporate and turn into white salt. We took two pecks of it for our use on the journey. Mounting in a south-easterly direction we reached the watershed and saw to the west of us a high ravine filled with what seemed to be ice, but was in fact merely salt. On the top of the ridge were red stones also composed of salt. The Master tasted them himself,

[1] Hui-ho.

and was struck by the fact that in the east salt is only found on low ground, while in these parts it also occurs in the mountains. The natives are very fond of cakes, with which they eat a great deal of salt. This makes them thirsty, and they drink a lot of water. It is no uncommon sight even in the depths of winter to see poor people selling water in pitchers.

On the fourteenth day (September 20th) we reached the foot of the mountains to the south-west of the Iron Gates. The last part of the pass is flanked by very high and precipitous cliffs. On the left side there had been a heavy landslide, which had completely buried the stream at the bottom of the valley for a distance of more than a mile.

On the day of mid-autumn (fifteenth of the eighth month) we came to a river—the Amu—which reminded us of the Yellow River. It flows to the north-west. We crossed it in a boat and camped on the southern bank. To the west there is a frontier-fort called T'uan-pa-la ; its situation in the mountains renders it very difficult to attack.

We now met on the road with Lord Chēng,[1] the personal physician of the Khan's third son (Ögödäi). The Master presented him with a poem.

[1] Chēng Ching-hsien, called Lung-kang (" Dragon Mound "). A close friend of Yeh-lü Ch'u-ts'ai, with whom he exchanged numerous poems. Highly valued by Ögödäi, who after his accession offered Ching-hsien several important posts in the government.

AN ALCHEMIST

We followed the river up-stream and then went south-east for thirty *li*. Lack of water now compelled us to travel by night. We passed the great city of Balkh.[1] Its inhabitants had recently rebelled against the Khan and been removed ;[2] but we could still hear dogs barking in its streets.

At dawn we breakfasted and after going eastward for twenty or thirty *li* came to a river that ran to the north. We were just able to ford it on horseback, and on the far side rested and camped for the night. On the twenty-second (September 28th) Chinkai came to meet us and we were soon in the Khan's camp.

Presently the Khan sent Chinkai to ask whether the Master wished to see him at once or to rest for a little first. The Master replied that he was ready. On this as on all subsequent occasions when Taoists interviewed the Emperor we did not kneel or bow down before him, but merely inclined the body and pressed the palms of the hands together on entering his tent. When the audience was over we were given kurmiss, and as soon as it was finished took our leave. The Emperor asked whether we were properly provided for at our lodging in Samarkand. The Master replied that previously the supplies received from the Mongols,

[1] Captured in 1220; destroyed in 1222, probably a few weeks before Ch'ang-ch'un's arrival.
[2] We know from Rashid-ed-din that after their "removal" they were put to the sword.

the natives and the Governor had been adequate, but that recently there had been some difficulties about food, the provision of which had fallen entirely upon the Governor. Next day the Emperor again sent his personal officers to our tent. He had asked him to suggest that the Adept should take all his meals with the Emperor. But the Master replied: " I am a mountain hermit and am only at my ease in quiet places ". The Emperor said he was to be humoured. On the twenty-seventh day the Emperor set out on his return to the north. On the way he sent us repeated presents of grape-wine, melons and greens.

On the first of the ninth month we crossed a bridge of boats and went on to the north. The Master now pointed out that the time for his discourse had arrived and suggested that the Governor A-hai should be summoned.[1]

On the fifteenth (October 1st) an imposing pavilion was erected, the women of the Khan's retinue were sent away. To left and right candles and torches flared. Only Chinkai, being a *chärbi*[2] and the envoy Liu Wēn were allowed even to be in attendance at the door. The Master entered accompanied by the Governor A-hai and A-li-hsien. After taking his seat he pointed out that Liu Wēn and Chinkai had performed immense journeys on his behalf and begged

---

[1] To act as interpreter.   [2] Chamberlain.

that they might be admitted, so that they too could hear his discourse. This suggestion was followed. The Master's words were translated into Mongo by A-hai. The Emperor was delighted with his doctrine and on the nineteenth, when there was a bright night, sent for him again. On this occasion too he was much pleased by what he heard, and sent for the Master to his tent once more on the twenty-third (October 29th). He was here treated with the same regard as before and the Emperor listened to him with evident satisfaction. He ordered that the Master's words should be recorded, and especially that they should be written down in Chinese characters, that they might be preserved from oblivion. To those present he said : " You have heard the holy Immortal discourse three times upon the art of nurturing the vital spirit. His words have sunk deeply into my heart. I rely upon you not to repeat what you have heard ". During the remainder of the Imperial Progress to the east, the Master constantly[1] discoursed to the Emperor concerning the mysteries of Tao.

A few days' travel brought us back to the great city of Samarkand, where we halted thirty *li* south-west of the town. On the first day of the tenth month (November 5th) the Master asked if he might return

[1] On November 19th he delivered the discourse summarized in my Introduction (p. 21) entitled *Hsüan Fēng* . . . *Lu.*

113

8

to his old lodging. This was allowed. The Emperor himself finally camped twenty *li* east of the town. On the sixth day of this month the Master went with A-hai into the Emperor's presence. Upon the Emperor asking whether those present must withdraw, the Master replied that there was no need for secrecy. He then made A-hai explain that he had led the life of a mountain recluse for so long that he had become used to the utmost quiet. To travel in the midst of the Imperial retinue, subjected to continual disturbance from the bustle and din of an army, was extremely vexatious to him and he begged that as a favour he might be allowed to travel always a little in front or behind. This too was accorded. When he was already outside the tent the Emperor sent some one after him to know whether he was in need of any cotton-stuff. The Master said that he did not need any.

At this season a fine rain begins to fall and the grass becomes green again. Then, after the middle of the eleventh month, the rain becomes heavier, sometimes turning to snow, and the ground becomes saturated. From the time of the Master's first arrival in Samarkand it was his habit to give what grain we could spare to the poor and hungry of the city. Often, too, he would send hot rice-meal, and in this way saved a great number of lives.

AN ALCHEMIST

On the twenty-sixth (December 30th) we set out. On the twenty-third of the twelfth month (January 26th, 1223) there was a snow-ſtorm and such intense cold that many oxen and horses were frozen to death on the road. After three days we crossed the Khojand-mürän[1] from weſt to eaſt and soon reached the Khan's camp. Here we learnt that on the twenty-eighth, in the middle of night, the bridge of boats had broken loose and been swept away.[2] The Khan asked the reason of calamities such as earthquakes, thunder and so on. The Maſter replied : " I have heard that in order to avoid the wrath of Heaven you forbid your countrymen to bathe in rivers during the summer,[3] wash their clothes, make fresh felt or gather mushrooms in the fields. But this is not the way to serve Heaven. It is said that of the three thousand sins the worſt is ill-treatment of one's father and mother. Now in this respeĉt I believe your subjeĉts to be gravely at fault and it would be well if your Majeſty would use your influence to reform them ".

[1] The Syr Darya.
[2] Immediately after Ch'ang-Ch'un crossed.
[3] One day when Chagatai and Ögödäi were hunting they saw a Moslem bathing in a ſtream. Chagatai was about to slay him when Ögödäi tossed a coin into the ſtream and whispered to the man to say that he had gone into the water to look for a loſt coin. These prohibitions are discussed by d'Ohsson, *Hiſtoire des Mongols*, Vol. I, end (1852 edition). They applied especially to the summer as being the season of thunder (i.e. God's wrath). The prohibition againſt making felt muſt here obviously be taken as referring to summer only. The prohibition againſt washing clothes was apparently absolute. They muſt be worn till they were in rags. This cuſtom, the objeĉt of which was to avoid offence to the water-spirits, is noted by Rubruck and Carpini. The anecdote quoted above is given by Wang Kuo-wei as though it came from d'Ohsson, where however I cannot find it.

This pleased the Khan and he said: "Holy Immortal, your words are exceedingly true; such is indeed my own belief", and he bade those who were present write them down in Uighur characters. The Master asked that what he had said might be made known to the Khan's subjects in general, and this was agreed to.

The Khan also summoned his sons and the other princes, high ministers and officers, and said to them: "The Chinese reverence this holy Immortal just as you revere Heaven; and I am more than ever convinced that he is indeed a Being from Heaven"! And he proceeded to repeat to them all that the Master had taught him on various occasions, adding: "Heaven sent this holy Immortal to tell me these things. Do you engrave them upon your hearts". The Master then retired.

On the first day of the New Year (February 2nd, 1223) the Chief Commander, the Chief Physician and the Chief Soothsayer all came to pay the compliments of the season. On the eleventh day we turned our horses' heads to the east, looking back for a moment towards Samarkand, already a thousand *li* or more behind us. We halted for a while in a large orchard. The nineteenth was the Master's birthday and all the officials burnt incense-candles and wished him long life. On the twenty-eighth Lord Li, Intendant in the Governor's office, came to say good-bye. Upon the Master's asking him whether his parting was indeed final, Li said that they would meet again in the third month. " You are ignorant ", said the Master, " of Heaven's decree. In the second or third month I return to China."

On the twenty-first day we went one stage eastwards and came to a great river.[1] From here to Sairam is about three stages. The place is very fertile and well-watered; so we stayed for some time in order to refresh our oxen and horses.

On the seventh day of the second month (March 9th) the Master had an Audience and told the Khan that he had promised to be back in three years and now that the third year had come he was impatient to be back in his mountain retreat. The Emperor replied : " I am myself on my way to the east. Will you not travel with me ? " The Master said he would rather go on ahead, for he had promised his friends in China to be back among them in three years. He had by now answered all the Khan's questions and earnestly desired to be dismissed. The Khan however wished him to stay for a few days more. " My sons ", he said, " are soon arriving. There are still one or two points in your previous discourses which are not clear to me. When they have been explained, you may start on your journey."

[1] Probably the Chirchik.

On the eighth (March 11th) the Khan went hunting in the mountains to the east. He shot a boar; but at this moment his horse stumbled and he fell to the ground. Instead of rushing upon him, the boar stood perfectly still, apparently afraid to approach. In a moment his followers brought him the horse, the hunt was stopped and they all returned to the camp. Hearing of this incident the Master reproached the Emperor, telling him that in the eyes of Heaven life[1] was a precious thing. The Khan was now well on in years and should go hunting as seldom as possible. His fall, the Master pointed out, had been a warning, just as the failure of the boar to advance and gore him had been due to the intervention of Heaven. " I know quite well ", replied the Emperor, " that your advice is extremely good. But unfortunately we Mongols are brought up from childhood to shoot arrows and ride. Such a habit is not easy to lay aside. However, this time I have taken your words to heart." Then turning to *Kishlik Darkan*[2] he said : " In future I shall do exactly as the holy Immortal advises ". It was indeed two months before he again went hunting.

[1] This has been generally taken to mean the Khan's life. But it is rather the boar's life that is referred to. Hunting was disapproved of by Buddhists and Taoists because it involved the taking of life. The Khan's age made it all the more urgent that he should mend his ways.

[2] The Kerait stallman who in 1203 had warned him of the Kerait Khan's intended treachery.

AN ALCHEMIST

On the twenty-fourth day the Master had another farewell interview. The Emperor said he was considering what to give him as a parting present and begged him to wait a little longer. The Master saw that it was impossible to start immediately and reluctantly agreed to wait. On the seventh of the third month he again attempted a farewell. The Emperor wished to make him a gift of oxen and horses, but he would not accept them, saying that he only required the usual post-horses. The Emperor on this occasion asked A-li-hsien, who was interpreting, whether the Master had many disciples in China. "A very great many", said A-li-hsien. "When I was escorting him from China we stopped at the Lung-yang Temple in Tē-hsing, and there I saw the tax-collector's lists of assessment." The Emperor then directed that the Master's pupils should henceforward be exempted from taxation, and he published an Edict[1] to the same effect, sealing it with the Imperial Seal.

A-li-hsien, as special envoy, was to accompany the Master on his journey home, supported by the Mongols Ho-la and Pa-hai. On the tenth day he had his final farewell with the Emperor, and set out. All the officers of the camp, from the *darkans* downward, accompanied him several miles, bearing presents of

[1] For the text, see below, p. 158.

grape-wine and rare fruits, and at parting all of them were obliged to brush away their tears.

We reached Sairam in three days. In the mountains to the south-east of this large town there is a serpent with two heads, about two feet long. The natives often see it. On the day of the full moon the Master's disciples went outside the town to sacrifice at the grave of Chao Chin-ku.[1] We were for taking his remains back with us, but the Master quoted the verses :

> A temporary compound of the Four Elements,
> The body at last must suffer decay.
> The soul, composed of one spiritual essence,
> Is free to move wherever it will.

This settled the discussion.

We set out again next day and on the twenty-third were overtaken by the envoy Yang A-kou, who had come to take leave of the Master ; they met on the southern banks of the river Chu. After ten days, about a hundred *li* west of Almalig, we crossed a big river,[2] and on the fifth of the fourth month (May 6th) reached the gardens east of the city of Almalig. Here Chang,[3] the chief artificer of the Khan's second son Chagatai, came to the Master with an urgent request. He said that near where he was living there were three altars which were visited for worship and prayer by more

---

[1] See above, p. 90.
[2] The Ili.
[3] Chang Jung, who built the bridge of boats over the Amu Darya. See his Life in *Tüan Shih* 151. He was a Shantung man.

than four hundred people every morning and evening.
He entreated the Master to reward so much zeal by
being so kind as to cross the river and accord to those
who crowded round the altars the supreme benefit of
his instruction ; there were still several days to spare.
The Master declined, saying that Fate had something
in store for him quite soon, upon the south side of the
river, and it was impossible for him to alter his course.
But on Chang repeating the request, he said he would
go unless some hindrance should intervene. Next day
the horse that the Master was riding bolted to the
north-east and his followers were unable to catch it.
Chang and the rest were much disheartened and wept,
saying that evidently their fate was not linked to his,
since an act of Heaven had carried him away from them.
In the evening we reached the foot of the Yin Shan and
there spent the night.   Next day we crossed the Forty-
eight Bridges and followed the stream for fifty *li* as far
as the Heavenly Lake.[1] After crossing the Yin Shan
in a north-easterly direction we travelled for twenty[2]
days and finally came out upon the post road previously
taken by us, where it follows the course of a great river
to the south of the Chin Shan.   We then crossed the
Chin Shan from north to south and followed the
course of the mountains in a north-easterly direction.

[1] Sairam Lake.
[2] The text says " two ", which is an evident misprint.

On the twenty-eighth day of the fourth month (May 29th), there was a heavy fall of rain and snow. Next day all the mountains were white. We continued to follow the course of the mountains north-east for three days and then reached the A-pu-han Mountains, where we were met by Sung Tao-an and the eight other disciples whom we had left here, together with the congregations of the Everlasting Springtide and Jade Flower,[1] as well as the envoy Kuo Tē-ch'üan, who brought us to the Ch'i-hsia temple. When the Master was alighting from the wagon, a second rain-storm began, which gave great satisfaction, the people explaining that in the summer they usually had very little rain. Even such thunder-showers as came generally fell only in the mountains to the north and south of them. They attributed the present downpour entirely to the Master's religious power.

In ordinary years the inhabitants are obliged to irrigate their fields and gardens by digging canals. The wheat begins to ripen in the eighth month, having been watered entirely by irrigation. The harvest is apt to be spoilt by field mice, which are generally white. The cold is here so great that fruits are very late in forming. The river bank, during the fifth month, is composed of earth to the depth of about a foot. But under this is a further foot of solid

---

[1] Communities of Taoist believers.

ice. Every day after dinner we used to send people to fetch us ice. To the south are high mountain ranges that are snow-covered even in the hotteſt weather. Concerning this diſtrict many ſtrange facts are reported. A little to the weſt, by the side of a lake, there is a "wind-tomb". It is covered with white clay in which there are a number of cracks. In the second and third months when the wind is about to rise in the ranges to the south, a ſtrange noise in these holes always gives warning beforehand of the approaching ſtorm. When the wind firſt comes from inside the "tomb" it seems to move spirally, like a ram's horn. Finally thousands of these small spirals unite in one whirlwind, which sends the duſt flying, rolls ſtones along the ground, uproots trees, blows off roofs, and beats upon the valleys till they shake. Then, retreating to the south-eaſt, it suddenly dies away.

Beside a torrent to the south-eaſt are three or four watermills. When the ſtream reaches level ground it gradually dries up and disappears. In the mountains there is a great deal of coal. To the eaſt are two springs which in the winter months suddenly burſt out, forming great rivers and lakes. For a while the water then runs underground, only to burſt out again further on, fish and all. Often it floods the people's houses and it is only in the second month of spring that the waters gradually recede and the ground can be dug.

Some thousand *li* to the north-west is the country of Chien-chien-chou,[1] where good iron is found, and squirrels' fur. Corn, too, is grown. Numerous Chinese workmen[2] are settled there, occupied in weaving fine silks, gauze, brocade and damask. The south-west of the temple looks towards the Chin-shan. These mountains get a great deal of rain and hail. Even in the fifth and sixth months the snow is often ten feet deep. In the country to the north there is a desert in which the orobanche grows. The local name for it is *söyän*. They call water *wusu* and grass *aipusu*.[3] Far up into the Yin Shan (?)[4] the pine-trees are all a hundred feet high.

The members of the congregations made the following address to the Master : " This district, lying far away from any civilized region, has never since the earliest days received instruction in the True Doctrine. The people have consequently been led astray into the worship of mountain-spirits and wood-demons. But since the foundations of this temple they have more than once celebrated the Festival of the Dead,[5] and on the first and fifteenth days of the month there have

[1] The region of the Upper Yenissei, north of the Tangnu-ola Mountains. The two branches of the river are still called Ulu Kem (Big River) and Kemchik (Rivulet). It formed the south-eastern part of the Kirghiz country. The " Kem-kemjiyūt " of Rashid-ed-din.

[2] In 1265 Kubilai Khan summoned to Peking a number of craftsmen from the City of Chinkai, from Pai-li-pa and Chien-chien-chou.

[3] The forms attested by the *Secret History* are *usun* and *äbäsü*.

[4] Certainly a misprint for *shan-yin*, " the sunless side ".

[5] The Chung-yüan festival on the 15th of the 7th month.

been regular meetings of the faithful. The rules against taking of life have been generally observed. Only the mysterious operation of Tao could have wrought such a change. Last year the Taoist community suffered much from the jealousy of certain evil men, and we had some unpleasant experiences. But one day, when Sung Tao-an had fallen asleep in his cell there suddenly appeared at a hole in the roof the figure of Chao Chin-ku,[1] who said : ' A letter has come '. ' Whence did it come ? ' asked Sung. ' From Heaven ', replied the apparition, and held out a letter, upon which seemed only to be written the two words ' Great Purity '. Then the letter and its bearer suddenly vanished. Next day your letter came, and since then our torments have gradually decreased. The physician Lo, who had worked against us in every possible way, one day fell from his horse right in front of our temple and broke his leg. He at once repented of his errors, saying that this accident had come as a punishment and begged the Taoists to forgive him ".

Before setting out to the east, the Master composed a set of instructive verses for the benefit of the community :

For ten thousand *li* I have rode on a Government horse,
It is three years since I parted from my friends.
The weapons of war are still not at rest ;

[1] See pp. 75, 90, 120, 131.

But of the Way and its workings I have had my chance to
preach.
On an autumn night I spoke of the management of breath ;
At Spring's end I approach my native land.
When I think of returning to those numberless crowds[1]
Deep in my heart are feelings too great to express.

A-li-hsien and the reſt now told him that the
southern route was very barren and ſtony. There was
indeed so little grass or water that large numbers of
travellers could not go at the same time without risk
of the horses collapsing, which would entail great delay.
The Maſter therefore agreed to split up his party into
three seſtions, and thus enable every one to travel in
greater comfort. On the seventh day of the fifth
month he sent on ahead Sung Tao-an, Hsia Chih-ch'ēng
Sung Tē-fang, Mēng Chih-wēn, Ho Chih-chien and
P'an Tē-chung. On the fourteenth he set out himself
with Yin Chih-p'ing, Wang Chih-ming, Yü Chih-k'o,
Chü Chih-yüan, Yang Chih-ching, and Ch'i Chih-
ch'ing.

Among those who saw him off, bringing farewell
offerings, was Chia-ku Fei,[2] the envoy Kuo, General Li
and others, making a score in all. They went with him
about twenty *li*, and then dismounting bowed twice
and took leave of him with tears in their eyes. The
Maſter whipped his horse and rode on quickly. On
the eighteenth day Chang Chih-su, Sun Chih-chin,

[1] i.e., of Taoiſt followers.
[2] Chia-ku was a common surname among the Kin Tartars.

AN ALCHEMIST

Chēng Chih-hsiu, Chang Chih-yüan and Li Chih-ch'ang followed. After travelling for sixteen days the Maßter crossed a great mountain. There was snow on it and the cold was intense. We changed horses at a *fu-lu.*[1] On the seventeenth day the Maßter ate nothing and only occasionally sipped a little soup. Going south-eaßtwards we crossed a great belt of sand, with, however, some grass and trees growing on it. It was much infeßted by gnats and flies. That night we lodged to the eaßt of a river and then continued for several days. The Maßter took to riding part of the time in a wagon inßtead of on his horse. Yin Chih-p'ing and others enquired what was the matter with him ; but he said his illness was not of the kind that physicians can underßtand, but was like the cutting and polishing of precious ßtones ; he would be the holier and wiser for it. " I cannot expeét to recover at present ", he told them, " but you must not worry about me ". His followers were however, very anxious about him. That night Yin Chih-p'ing dreamt that a divine being came to him and said : " You need not be worried about the Maßter's illness. He will recover as soon as he sets foot on Chinese soil".

We followed a track over the sands for over three hundred *li.* There was hardly any paßture or water,

---

[1] Tibetan *pu-lu*, a rough shelter of ßtones or skins. The word occurs in Chinese from the T'ang dynaßty onwards. Laufer (*T'oung Pao*, 1914, p. 92, and 1916, p. 534) suggests a different derivation.

so that the horses had to press straight on all through
the night without any rest. But by the second night
we had come out of the desert at a place near the
northern frontier of the Tangut country. Here
already there were more huts and tents and we had no
difficulty in getting fresh horses. The Master's party
was caught up by those behind, and on the twenty-
second of the sixth month (July 21st) we spent the
night at the Yü-yang Barrier.[1] The Master had still
eaten nothing. Next day we went through the
Barrier, and fifty *li* to the east arrived at Fēng-chou.[2]
Everyone, from the Commander down, came to meet
us and the envoy Yü asked the Master to stay in his
house. Upon hot cakes being served the Master
immediately ate a great many of them, and later at
dinner he ate and drank as usual. The Taoists said
to one another that Yin Chih-p'ing's dream was now
fulfilled. It was now late in the summer, but a cool
wind blew on to the verandah at the back of the house.
While the Master was sitting here Yü brought him some
specially soft paper, upon which he wrote a poem. On
the first day of the seventh month (July 30th, 1223) we
set out again and after three days reached the Lower
Water[3] and here the Commander Chia-ku[4] came out

[1] North of the modern Kukukhoto.
[2] Near Kukukhoto.
[3] The modern Taiha-nor.
[4] Chia-ku T'ung-chu, at that time Governor of Shansi province. By birth
a Kin Tartar.

from the town[1] to meet us and made the Master his guest at the house where he lodged. Certainly as many as a thousand persons came to do him homage, and the Governor himself became every day more reverential. He presented the Master with three captured wild-geese. On the evening of the seventh day the Master made an excursion outside the town and set them free on the lake. He watched them for a little while dart and play amid the windy waves in manifest delight at their freedom. He made the following poem :

They tended you to no purpose, save to bring you to the
    kitchen ;
And only my kind intent saved you from becoming a meal.
In light skiff I took you out and set you among the huge waves
There to wait till at autumn's end your wings are fully grown.

Next day we set out and on the ninth day of the month arrived in Yün-chung (Ta-t'ung Fu). The Envoy-in-General-Control A-pu-ho, with many Taoists came outside the town to meet the Master and brought him back to his own house in a carrying-chair. Here he remained for over twenty days, lodging in an upper room. A-pu-ho and the officials under him came every morning and evening to pay him their respects, while the nobles and dignitaries of the place came daily to seek his instruction. On the thirteenth the

[1] From Ta-t'ung Fu.

envoy A-li-hsien, when about to go to Shantung with proclamations, was anxious to take the disciple Yin Chih-p'ing with him. The Master answered: "Heaven has not yet indicated such a step. What will be gained by his going?" A-li-hsien, bowing once more, explained that if the Khan were to arrive with a large army the "sacred spirit of life" would certainly be exposed to carnage. A word from the Master himself might be the means of saving those in danger. After much hesitation the Master admitted that it was better to fail in an effort to save life than simply to sit by and watch the slaughter. He therefore sent Yin with the envoy, entrusting him with two proclamations.[1] He heard, too, that a great number of Taoists from south of Hsüan-tē[2] were gathering to meet him, and, fearing that the entertainment of them would overtax the resources of the Taoist monasteries, he asked Yin to deal with them, giving him an autograph letter in which he said: "I have been absent three years on end, covering in my long journey a distance of many thousand *li*. A certain number of Taoists have in the interval shown themselves to be unruly and without principle. I invest Yin Chih-p'ing with full authority to deal with such wherever he finds them, lest the disciples of Tao should themselves

---

[1] Recommending an unequivocal surrender to the Mongols.
[2] Now Hsüan-hua Fu.

impede its mysterious power. The prosperity of mortal creatures is a most uncertain thing. How easily it slips away! Just as the hill that was so hard to climb is descended with only too little effort or exertion ".

The Commander of Hsüan-tê, the lord Yeh-lü (I-la) sent a special messenger to Yün-chung offering the Master his own horse to ride on, and at the beginning of the eighth month we set out to the east, through Yang-ho, Po-têng and Huai-an.[1] We crossed the river Hun,[2] and arrived at Hsüan-tê on the twelfth. The Commander met us in great state some way west of the town, and brought us to the Ch'ao-hsüan Kuan, the chief temple of the district. Here the people told him that last winter they had seen the disciple Chao Chin-ku come in at the gate leading a horse. When they went out to welcome him, he suddenly disappeared. He had also been seen at Tê-hsing and An-ting. Invitations now began to come in from princes, officials, generals and people of all sorts high and low, from every town and city north of the Yellow River, entreating the Master to accept their hospitality. This went on without a moment's pause, letter flashing after letter like the spokes of a revolving wheel. Generally he merely replied in a few words.

[1] Yang-ho is the modern Yang-kao hsien.
[2] The Yang-ho of modern maps.

131

On the firſt day of the tenth month (October 26th) he performed the service of the new moon at Lung-mēn-ch'uan.[1] On the day of the full moon he celebrated the rites at the Ch'ao-hsüan Kuan in Hsüan-tē itself. On the fifteenth of the eleventh month Sung Tē-fang and some others, in fulfilment of the vow made by them when we crossed the Yeh-hu Range,[2] and the bones of those who had died in battle, went with Miſtress Yin Ch'ien-i and said a Mass in the Lung-yang Kuan at Tē-hsing on behalf of the lonely dead. For some time it had been very cold, but while the services were going on, for two nights and three days, it suddenly became as warm as in spring. After the service was over the Commander Chia Ch'ang arrived from the Khan's camp, bringing the following message : " Holy adept, between the spring and summer you have performed no easy journey. I wish to know whether you were properly supplied with provisions and remounts. At Hsüan-tē and the other places where you have lately ſtayed, did the officials make satisfaĉtory provision for your board and lodging ? Have your appeals to the common people resulted in their coming over to you ? I am always thinking of you and I hope you do not forget me ".

He celebrated the full moon of the twelfth month (January 7th, 1224) in the San Kuan ("Three

[1] Near Hsüan-hua Fu.   [2] See above, p. 62.

AN ALCHEMIST

Hostels ")[1] at Yü-chou.[2] During the winter he spent at the Lung-yang the Master used every morning and evening to go for a walk on the Dragon Mound. From here he had a view of the villages near Tē-hsing that had been devastated during the war, and made two poems on the subject.

In the second month of next year (1224) he performed the service of the new moon at the Ch'iu-yang Kuan at Chin-shan.[3] The temple is on the southern slopes of the Ko-shan. The landscape is here of surpassing beauty. The woods of pine-trees, hung with creepers, make it, when there is mist or moonlight, a true home for Taoists.

The Governor of Peking, his lordship Shih-mo,[4] on whom had been bestowed the order of the Gold and Purple, also the plenipotentiary Liu Min,[5] and their junior colleagues now sent a messenger with a letter[6] urgently begging the Master to take up his residence in the Ta T'ien-ch'ang Kuan at Peking. He consented, and it was arranged that he should travel by post. He went through Chü-yung and then turned south. His Taoist friends from Peking came out to

[1] Apparently the name of a Taoist temple.
[2] On the borders of Shansi and Chihli, almost due west of Peking.
[3] The modern Yen-ch'ing Chou; his disciple Yin-Chih-p'ing was staying at this temple.
[4] See above, p. 53.
[5] See below, p. 134.
[6] Dated August-September, 1223. The fifth of the documents printed as a supplement to the text.

meet him near Nan-k'ou, at the temple of Shēn-yu. Next morning a great gathering of the faithful, including people of all kinds from aged men to young women, escorted him into Peking with incense and garlands. The spectators were so numerous that they blocked the road. When he set out for the West he had told his followers that he should be away for three years, and now his words were fulfilled. On the first seventh day[1] he entered the T'ien-ch'ang Kuan. The number of persons who sat down to supper with him here every day was over a thousand. On the fifteenth the congregation invited him to the Yü-hsü Kuan. On the twenty-second Ho-la arrived from the Khan's camp with the following message : " Holy adept, now that you are in China, convert the people with your pure doctrine, and each day recite the scriptures on my behalf and pray that I may live long. Your noble teaching should be set in excellent surroundings. Establish yourself where you would best like to live. I have told A-li-hsien that you are now very old and that he is to be very careful of you. Do not forget what I told you before ". In the fifth month the Governor of Peking and Liu Min[2] several times sent letters begging him to take over the direction of the Ta T'ien-ch'ang Kuan, and on the twenty-second day

---

[1] The seventh day of the first month (January 28th, 1224).

[2] Biography, *Yüan Shih* 153. He was a native of Hsüan-tē, but took service with the Mongols and became Governor of Hsüan-tē.

he returned there and did as they suggested. Several cranes flew in front of him and then disappeared to the north-west. When he was at the Yü-hsü Kuan and someone asked him out to supper, several cranes once flew over his head uttering loud cries. In Northern China there have never been many Taoists, and now the divinities, wishing to impress the multitude, had shown themselves in the form of cranes. The members of all the eight congregations all bowed and knelt down before him, paying him Taoist homage. There was indeed a change in the whole attitude of the people towards Taoism. The water in the well at the Yü-hsü Kuan had long been brackish. But in the years *Chia-shēn* and *I-yu*[1] when there were collected here all the Taoists who had returned from the west, the water suddenly became sweet in taste. This, too, arose from the general trend towards piety.

On the fifteenth of the sixth month (July 3rd) the envoy Chancellor Ja'far[2] brought the message from the Khan : " Since you went away, I have not once forgotten you for a single day. I hope you do not forget me. If there is anywhere in my whole dominions where you would particularly like to be, you have only to say so, and shall live there. I wish

[1] 1224, 1225.
[2] Ja'far Khoja, apparently a native of Yanikant, near the mouth of the Syr Darya. For his biography see *Yüan Shih* 120, where the name of his birthplace is given as Sai-i. This is probably a mistake for Yang-i (i.e., Yanikant). The *Mēng Ta Pei Lu* (1221 A.D.) already speaks of him as an " aged man ". He lived to be 118 !

your disciples to recite the scriptures continually on my behalf and to pray for my longevity ".

Ever since the Master's return Taoists had been assembling in huge numbers from every direction and the opponents of our religion became every day less active. In the Capital there was a general conversion to the faith and its tenets became household words ; so that the gates of our doctrine were opened to the four quarters of the earth in a manner never before witnessed. At the T'ien-ch'ang eight congregations were founded, named : P'ing-tēng (" Equality "), Ch'ang-ch'un (" Everlasting Spring "), Ling-pao (" Magic Jewel "), Ch'ang-shēng (" Everlasting Life "), Ming-chēn (" Bright Purity "), P'ing-an (" Peace and Safety "), Hsiao-tsai (" Dispel Calamity ") and Wan-lien (" Ten Thousand Lilies ").

After his return to the T'ien-ch'ang Kuan the number of Taoists who came from distant parts to receive religious names daily increased. Every day after supper he would take a walk in an old garden on the Ch'iung-hua Island.[1] Here with six or seven followers he would sit in the shade of the pine-trees, himself making poems which the others in turn would match with compositions in the same rhyme-scheme.

---

[1] In what had been the Imperial gardens of the Kin dynasty ; they occupied part of the same ground as the modern Forbidden City. See *Cho Kēng Lu*, XXI, 8 verso. Also, Bouillard, *Historique du Territoire de Peking* (Bulletin of Stockholm Museum of Far Eastern Antiquities, No. 1), Map 2.

AN ALCHEMIST

After tea had been served he would make his followers
sing a few ballads to the tune and metre of *The Wandering Hsien.* Sunset would already be gleaming on the
mountains; but he, carried away by the beauty of the
spot, would forget the lateness of the hour. The
Governor and Ja'far now offered to present him with
the lake, garden and twenty or thirty *mou*[1] of ground
to the north of the Palace. They further requested
that he would found a Taoist temple there. At first
he refused, but upon a second request he allowed
himself to be persuaded. Notices were accordingly
put up that no one was to gather firewood there.
Taoist priests were installed and the work of construction
and repair grew every day more active. The Khan
was informed of what had been done, and signified his
approval. Henceforward there was not a fine day
upon which the Master did not come here to take his
walks.

In the fourth month of the year I-yu[2] the Controller
lord Wang Chü-ch'uan,[3] who was a Shensi man, asked
the Master to supper. They naturally fell to talking
of the marvellous bamboo thickets on Mount Chung-
nan near Hsien-yang.[4] Wang asked the Master to
inspect the bamboos in his courtyard. The Master
said they were particularly fine, and that after the

[1] About five acres?   [2] 1225.
[3] The Wang Chi mentioned above, p. 54.
[4] Modern Si-an Fu.

devaftation of the recent wars not many such had probably survived. He related that he had himself once lived at P'an-ch'i, a place famous throughout China for the greenness of its woods and the length of its bamboos. " When I looked back on those days at P'an-ch'i ", the Mafter said, " they seem like a dream. Now I am growing old and the time for my Departure is drawing near. Give me a few score of these bamboos to plant outside the northern verandah of the Pao-hsüan, to keep the light from my eyes." The Controller answered : " The war is ftill undecided. The people are in great suspense. It happens that the Khan has a great respect for you and sets ftore by the Taoift religion. By the ftrength of your holy Tao lives might be saved. This is no time to speak of your Departure. You should rather be thinking of how to show compassion to those who are in need of your help ". The Mafter banged his ftaff on the ground and laughed, saying : " The will of Heaven is fixed. What can man do ? " Those present did not at the time underftand his meaning.[1]

At the end of the fifth month he climbed the Shou-lo Hill,[2] whence gardens and woods are to be seen on every side, spread out like green tents under which the wanderer may rest safe from the summer heat. On

---

[1] Did not underftand the reference to his approaching death.
[2] The modern Tsung Shan.

this subject he made a Regular Poem in the five-word metre.

One day when he was returning from the Ch'iung-hua Island Ch'ēn Hsiu-yü came to speak to him. The Master showed him a Regular Poem in the seven-word metre. On the first of the ninth month (October 4th) the Controller Wang Chi came to the Master pointing out that the planet Mars had impinged upon the constellation Wei[1] to which corresponded the district of Peking. A calamity was bound to follow, and he begged the Master to perform a service in order to avert this danger. He also asked how much such a service would cost. He replied : " I could not bear to stand by and see one single object needlessly destroyed ; how much the less then could I haggle, where the safety of a whole district is at stake ? In recent years the people have been subject to such heavy exactions that all resources both private and public are well-nigh exhausted. I am quite willing to perform the service with such materials as lie to hand in my monastery. All I ask of you is to order the Officials of the Capital to fast and keep themselves pure until the rite has been performed ". It was accordingly arranged that the service should last for two whole days and nights. Despite his great age the

---

[1] A constellation in Scorpio. The Chinese believed that every point on earth corresponded to and was influenced by a related point in the heavens.

Master himself officiated at the Mysterious Altar. When the second night's service was over the Controller Wang Chi came to congratulate him, saying, that the planet was now several mansions away, and that the danger was past, so swiftly had the Master's magic taken effect. " What is this about magic ? " said the Master. " Prayer is no new thing. All that is needed is to believe in it. This is what the ancients meant when they said : ' Absolute belief could move the sky and the earth ' ". On the ninth day of the ninth month (October 12th) a large number of Taoists came from distant places with offerings of chrysanthemum-flowers. He made for them a poem in lines of unequal length, to the tune *Yü Shēng Hēn Huan Ch'ih*.

One day there was a dispute and the Master was asked which side he took. He remained silent, and thus settled the question in accordance with the spirit of Tao. Presently he gave them the following hymn :

Sweep, sweep, sweep !
Sweep clear the heart till there is nothing left.
He with a heart that is clean-swept is called a " good man ".
A " good man " is all that is meant by " holy *hsien* " or " *Fo* ".[1]

The disputants retired discomfited. In the first month of the year Ping Hsü (1226) the community at

---

[1] The *hsien* (highest being of Taoism) and the *Fo*, i.e., Buddha (highest being of Buddhism) are simply " good men " ; they do not belong to a separate order of beings.

AN ALCHEMIST

P'an-shan[1] asked him to come and perform the service of the Yellow Book for three nights and days. The day when the ceremonies began was unusually fine and every one was in high spirits. In the cold valleys signs of spring were already beginning to appear.

In the fifth month there was a great drought in the Capital. The farmers could not sow and a disaster was foreseen. The authorities cleared the markets and set altars up in them. Prayers were offered week after week, but with no result. The Governor sent an envoy to the Master begging him to pray for rain. He performed the rites for three days and two nights, and on the night when the holy figures[2] were to be prayed to, clouds suddenly gathered on all sides, and rain began to fall, continuing from midnight till breakfast time next day. The Governor sent a messenger who burnt incense and tendered the thanks of the City, saying that the drought had nearly burnt up the fields, corn had not been sown and the people had small hope of surviving. But thanks to the magic power of the Master, the Pure Ones Above had been moved to pour down sweet balm upon the people, who with one accord called it " The Adept's Rain ". " This effect ", answered the Master, " was produced

---

[1] N.E. of Peking. The remains of a Buddhist temple, destroyed during the campaign of the Mongols against the Kin Tartars, had been seized by Ch'ang-ch'un's disciple Ch'i-yün-tzŭ and turned into a Taoist temple.

[2] Figures of Taoist deities and patriarchs.

by the Absolute Faith of His Excellency the Governor.
What power have I to cause the Holy Ones above to
show compassion and give the people life ? "

A second messenger now came saying that though a
certain amount of rain had fallen, it was not nearly
enough to make up for so long a drought. A real
downpour was needed. The Master said there was no
need to worry. When the powers above had once
been moved by Absolute Faith, they would not fail
faithfully to repay. A heavy rain must be close at
hand.

Sure enough, before the evening meal was over
floods of rain began to stream down. The harvest
was excellent, and various celebrities and scholars came
with poems in which they congratulated the Master.

He wrote the following inscription on a painting
of the *hsien* Tē-i, Yüan-pao and Hsüan-su by the
artist Chih Chung-yüan[1] :

Of those Holy Beings who have obtained Tao how little the
    world knows !
In what age did these three *hsien* manifest their hidden power ?
Of fearless teaching to the Powers of the Land they handed
    down the rule ;
They passed their time in the midst of the world, yet remote
    as Ch'ih-sung.[2]

[1] Flourished about 934 A.D. Native of Fēng-hsiang in Shensi, famous for his
Taoist pictures.
[2] An ancient *hsien*.

AN ALCHEMIST

When, at the invitation of the Governor and other authorities at Peking, the Master first came to the T'ien-ch'ang Temple he found both the image-halls and dwelling-rooms in a sad state of decay. Everywhere roofs were leaking and floors had fallen in. Windows, doors and stairs were in complete dilapidation. He told his disciples to do what they could day by day to repair the place, and gradually leaks were stopped, tottering walls shored up, until in the year Ping-hsü (1226) the whole building was thoroughly renovated. In addition to this, forty new cells were built. The whole work was carried out with such resources as the monks had on the spot, without any help from outside. During the summer no lamps were allowed to be lit in the refectory and the rule was only gradually relaxed at the end of Autumn. This was in order to guard against fire.

In the tenth month he left the Pao-hsüan wing to go and live in the Fang-hu. Every day he would send for Taoist masters, range them about him according to their eminence and discourse with them on abstruse topics. Often this went on all night. On the thirteenth day of the eleventh month at midnight he shook his garments, got up and walked in the courtyard. Then coming back to his seat he showed a Regular Poem in the five-word metre to his assembled followers.

In the year Ting-hai (1227) there was again a great drought lasting from spring till summer. The authorities repeatedly offered up prayers, but with no result at all. The Taoist congregations in the City came one day and begged the Master to perform the rain-bringing service, and subsequently the Hsiao-tsai[1] and other guilds made the same request.

The Master said quietly : " I was just thinking of celebrating such a service. That you, sirs, should have come with the same suggestion is an example of what is called 'spontaneous identity of ideas'. There remains nothing for it but that you, gentlemen of both persuasions,[2] should devote all your energy to the arrangements ".

It was accordingly agreed to hold the rain service on the first day of the fifth month and to begin the thanksgiving for rain on the third day. If, before the expiration of these three days, rain fell, it was to be accounted an answer to our prayers ; but if it fell after the three days it was not to be considered anything to do with the service. Someone said that it was impossible to foretell Heaven's purpose, and tried to persuade the Master that such an announcement was

---

[1] A Buddhist guild, devoted to the reciting of the Hsiao-tsai ('dispel calamity') charm ? See the scripture numbered 1010 in Nanjio's Catalogue of the Tripitaka. Takakusu (Taishō Edition : Vol. 19, p. 337). It is perhaps by mistake that this guild is mentioned above as having been founded by Ch'ang-ch'un. Here it certainly seems to be contrasted with the Taoist foundations.

[2] This phrase, misunderstood by Palladius, makes it clear that both Buddhist and Taoist deputations had come.

very impolitic. If by any chance the rain came at the wrong time, ill-disposed persons would certainly try to turn the incident to his discredit. " You do not know what you are talking about ", the Master replied. And sure enough as the time for the service arrived, rain fell all day, and by next day a foot of it had fallen. On the third day the weather cleared completely, and the thanksgiving service was performed exactly as he had foretold.

The weather now began to be uncomfortably hot. The Commander Chang Tzŭ-yün invited the Master to make an excursion with him to the western hills, and after refusing two or three times, he went. On the day after his arrival, when supper was over and a shower of rain had stopped, they walked over to the Tung-shan temple. Here he and the other guests sat in the woods. At dusk, when they were about to go home, he wrote and showed to those about him the following poem :

> On the western hills the air is fresh and pure ;
> After the rain the light clouds gleam,
> With fellow-guests in a pleasant wood I sit,
> Unheeded the Tao ripens and grows.

The Commander (Chang Tzŭ-yün) then invited him back to his house, where he passed several days. Crowds came here to listen to his teaching, and did not retire to rest till far on into the night. He then accepted an invitation at the Ta-ku temple ; and next day went on to the Ch'ing-mēng. On the evening of that day heavy rain came up from the north and there was a moſt alarming thunderſtorm which seemed to fill the whole sky with blaze and din. The Maſter said : " This is an application of Tao. Some man who has obtained Tao is flashing upon us his majeſtic light. It cannot be otherwise. Ordinary thunder and lightning are not like this ".

It was very late before the gueſts scattered. The Maſter lay down to reſt in a humble thatched room. Presently there was a violent squall of wind and rain, and a clap of thunder so loud that the doors and windows were shaken almoſt to bits. But in a moment the noise completely ſtopped. Every one was surprised at this, for thunder usually grows louder and louder, and does not come in one huge clap, only to disappear. But to this someone replied that the presence of a holy man in the place had overawed the God of Thunder.

On the twenty-fifth day of the fifth month, when he was back again at his own monaſtery, the Taoiſt Wang Chih-ming arrived from Ch'in-chou[1] with Imperial orders that the " hsien Island " in the northern palace should henceforward be called " The Palace of Ten Thousand Tranquillities ", and that the

[1] In Kansu, then part of the Tangut territory. It was at this moment that Chingiz, having completed the conquest of the Tanguts, returned to Mongolia.

AN ALCHEMIST

T'ien Ch'ang temple should be called the Ch'ang-ch'un (" Everlasting Spring ") Palace. All priests and persons of religion in the whole Empire were to be under the Master's control and he was to have the Golden Tiger Tally.[1] He was to be absolute over all the affairs of the Taoist community. After the Lesser Heats there were several spells of heavy rain and the heat grew much more intense.

Since the Ch'iung-hua Island had become part of the Taoist precincts no firewood had been gathered there nor fish caught. So that in the course of these years the number of birds in the gardens and fishes in the lake had become very great. The place thus became, in season, a favourite resort for those who wished to take the air.

In his spare time the Master went for a ride on his horse at least once a day; but on the twenty-first of the sixth month he was not well and stayed at home, bathing in the stream just to the east of the temple. On the twenty-third, someone announced that between the hours *ssŭ* and *wu*, during a great storm of thunder and rain, the southern bank of the T'ai-i lake[2] had collapsed and the water had all run out into the Eastern Lake, with a roar that was audible a score of *li* away. All the turtles, water-lizards and fish had been washed

[1] See above, p. 48.
[2] In the grounds of the Kin Imperial Palace; made by the Emperor Chang Tsung (ruled 1190-1209).

away, and the T'ai-i was completely dried up. The
hill at the northern outlet of the canal[1] had also
collapsed. Hearing of this the Master at first remained
silent, but after a time he said smiling : " When the
hills fall and the lakes dry up, is it not time for me to
go the same way ? " On the fourth day of the seventh
month he said to his disciples : " Tan-yang[2] once
prophesied to me, saying : ' After my death our
religion will see a great triumph. All parts of the
world, far and near on every side, will become homes
of the Tao. You shall witness this. Our temples will
be re-named by Imperial Command, and you yourself will preside over a huge monastery. Moreover a
messenger will come bearing a tally and laying upon
you the charge of all religious matters. That will
be the moment at which the fame of your good works
will be at its height ; and it will also be the moment
of your Return to Rest '. Now all Tan-yang's words
are fulfilled, like the joining of a severed tally. And
indeed I have no cause for anxiety, with such excellent
followers of our Faith ready here and elsewhere to
take control ". He had already shown signs of sickness
in the Pao-hsüan hall. In one day he was obliged to
go several times to the closet. His disciples wanted to
save him this exertion, but he would not let them,

[1] The " River of Golden Waters ", see *Cho Kēng Lu* XXI, 9 recto.
[2] Ma Yü, author of Nos. 1044, 1128, 1130, 1135 and 1136 in the Taoist Canon,
Wieger Catalogue.

AN ALCHEMIST

saying : " I do not like to give trouble. I fear you
ftill make diftinctions. What real difference is there
between a privy and a bed-room ? " On the seventh
day of the seventh month his disciples begged him to
show himself to the people, saying that every day a
great number of pious guefts sat down with the monks
to supper and would account it a great act of kindness
if only he would comfort them by a glimpse of him.
He promised to go into the refectory on the ninth day
(Auguft 22nd). On that day, in the afternoon, he
made the following set of valedictory verses :

Life and Death are but like morning and evening ;
The transient foam comes and vanishes ; but the ftream goes
    on untroubled.
Where through a chink light appears, one can jump over the
    Crow and Hare,[1]
When their magic power is fully disclosed they embrace the
    mountains and seas.
It reaches the remoteft corners of the earth as though they
    were a foot away ;
It breathes upon the myriad things as though it were the key-
    spring of Life.
These random words that my brush forms themselves will turn
    to duft,
Falling into the hands of worldly men who will not underftand
    them aright.

He then went up to the Pao[2]-hsüan hall and
returned to Purity. A ftrange perfume filled the room.

[1] The sun and moon.
[2] Other texts read Kuang-hsüan.

His disciples, with incense burners in their hands, came to perform their farewell obeisances. The people wanted to set up a lamentation, but the Master's personal attendants Chang Chih-su, Wu Chih-lü and the rest put a stop to this, and told them that the Master had just made a testament in which he had placed the disciple Sung Tao-an in general charge of the religion. He was to be assisted by Yin Chih-p'ing. Chang Chih-sung was to come next and Wang Chih-ming was to retain his direction of domestic arrangements. Sung Tē-fang, Li Chih-ch'ang and some others were to form a council and advise on affairs of religion. They then showed the Master's valedictory poem.

When this had been read, the Director Sung Tao-an and the other officers bowed twice and assumed their new appointments. At dawn hemp garments were donned and the rites of mourning carried out. By now some ten thousand people had hastened to the spot, to join in the ceremonies. The envoy Liu Wēn soon heard what had happened and said with a deep sigh : " From the moment the Adept came into the Khan's presence it was clear that as sovereign and subject they fitted one another perfectly. After they parted the Khan felt the greatest affection for him and never showed any signs of forgetting him. I must lose no time in informing His Majesty that the Master has already made his Ascent ".

AN ALCHEMIST

After the first seven days had elapsed vast numbers of Taoist priests and laymen arrived from every quarter to mourn for the Master, and their emotion was as great as if they had lost their own parents. The number of those who asked for instructions and the granting of religious names grew daily greater. About this time the Director Sung Tao-an said to Li Chih-ch'ang : " On the seventh of this month you and I both received the instructions of the Master that the giving of religious names could be delegated. The document might be written by us, provided that it bore a seal reproducing his handwriting. This arrangement has now been in practice for some time, and it will be best to continue it ".

About this time Yin Chih-p'ing came back[1] from Tē-hsing to carry out the prayers. When they were over and the last of the seven weeks of mourning was come the Director Sung Tao-an said to Yin Chih-p'ing : " I am too old to undertake the administration of the Faith. You must act in my name ". After twice declining, Yin accepted the charge, and under his care the Taoist congregations far and near continued steadily to grow in the number of their devoted adherents.

At the beginning of the third month in the spring of the year *mou-tzŭ* (1228) Yin Chih-p'ing proposed that a hall in memory of the Master should be built at

[1] See above, p. 130.

the White Clouds temple. Some said that such a work would make too heavy a demand upon their resources, both in material and labour, and would be impossible to carry to a conclusion. But Yin replied; " The chief essential in all undertakings is that someone should plan them out beforehand. The mass of people will gladly help in carrying out a plan, but will not take the trouble to think anything out beforehand. In this case, the undertaking is not a private one. We can rely on the resources of the whole Taoist community, and it is beyond question that the thing can somehow be managed. Moreover, the *hsien* our Master has left behind him the memory of his magic powers and there is not a place in the land where he is not devoutly admired. Even if we make no appeal for funds, we shall certainly receive assistance, so that on this head you need have no misgivings. And if by any chance sufficient help is not forthcoming—if we exhaust our own stocks of material and have come to the end of the temple-funds—all we have to do is to go round with a gourd-bowl. We can collect as much money as we please ".

The envoy-plenipotentiary Liu Wēn was delighted when he heard of the plan and did everything in his power to assist it, giving orders to Chü Chih-yüan and others to take over the direction of the work.

The clearing of the ground and laying of foundations

AN ALCHEMIST

began on the *ting*[1] day at the beginning of the first month. After the lapse of the three days *mou, ssŭ* and *kĕng*, there suddenly arrived a band of some two hundred Taoists from P'ing-yang, T'ai-yüan, Chien, Tai, Yü[2] and Ying, offering both funds and manual assistance for the building of the new temple. In forty days[3] the work was finished. It would be impossible to mention here the names of all those who in one way and another assisted in the performance of this pious work. Those best qualified to judge maintained that although the actual work of construction was carried out by human hands, it could never have been completed so rapidly without the secret intervention of the Holy and Wise Spirits. The burial of the *hsien* our master was fixed for the ninth day of the seventh month.[4] Such heavy rain fell during the sixth month that it was feared the burial would be delayed, but on the first of the seventh month it was suddenly announced that the weather showed signs of clearing, which was a great relief to all concerned. The day before the ceremonies began incense-burners were lighted, mats spread and everything done to invest the service with proper dignity. When the coffin was opened the

[1] The first day. These cyclical terms are here used as being appropriate to the geomantic-astrological calculations used in connection with the construction of buildings.
[2] This town is in Chihli; the rest in Shansi.
[3] The "four months" of Wang Kuo-wei's text is a misprint.
[4] The anniversary of his death. For a more detailed account of the funeral, see the *Kan Shui Hsien Yüan Lu* (Wieger, 965), ch. IX, fol. 6.

153

Master's face was found to be as full of expression as if he were still alive. For three days the coffin was left open and the remains were viewed by a vast concourse of princes, officials, scholars, commoners, Buddhist priests and nuns, Taoists and what not, from every part of the country. At least ten thousand visitors came on each of those three days, and all touched their foreheads with their hands as homage to the miracle displayed before them. The news spread rapidly; conversions to our Faith took place on every hand and innumerable pilgrims arrived at the coffin-side with lamps and incense-burners in their hand. The lying-in-state took place in the Master's own temple,[1] and lasted for three nights and days. It was preceded by ten days' fasting. On the eighth day at the hour of the Dragon (8 a.m.) a dark-coloured crane flew from the south-west, followed soon afterwards by a white crane.[2] All eyes were turned to the sky in wonder at this portent. On the ninth day at the hour of the Rat (midnight) the ritual Ling Pao Ch'ing[3] was performed and then the ritual of the Three Hundred and Sixty Locations.[4] When this was over the *hsien's* discarded husk was laid in the newly-built hall, which

---

[1] The T'ien-Ch'ang Kuan, now called, in obedience to Chingiz's command, the Ch'ang-ch'un Kung.

[2] The two cranes represented the Master's *po* (astral body) and *hun* (soul).

[3] Ling Pao ("Magic Treasure") is the second person of the Taoist Trinity. The rite in question was a sort of Mass for the Dead.

[4] The 360 spirits who dominate the days of the year.

for more than an hour afterwards was filled with a ſtrange fragrance. Towards noon dinner was served to several thousand wearers of the yellow cap and feather mantle.[1] There were also present over ten thousand lay members of our Faith. On the day after the Reposing of the Soul the rain began once more to fall heavily. This coincidence was noted, and it was generally remarked that the cessation of rain at the moment when this great ceremony began and its return when the ceremony was over, argued an extraordinary correspondence between the dispositions of Heaven and the convenience of man. Such a ſtate of harmony could only have been produced by the Maſter's spiritual power, which operated with equal force in heaven or earth, among the divine or the dead. Certainly no human influence could have sufficed to arrange matters thus.

The Temporary Provincial Governor and Commissioner Wang Chi came of a subſtantial family in Hsien-yang. He had long been intereſted in the Dark Wind (Taoism), and recently had been much in the Maſter's company at Peking. There was a remarkable identity between their taſtes and religious leanings. Wang in these days conceived a deep admiration for the Maſter, far exceeding what he had felt on the occasion of their previous intercourse. It was accordingly

[1] i.e., Taoiſts.

155

natural that he should preside over the burial. He guarded the Capital both inside and outside the walls with armed troops to deal with every disturbance, and the vast crowds dispersed without the slightest trace of panic or disorder.

Soon afterwards Wang Chi gave the dwelling-quarters of the temple the name Dwelling in Obedience inscribed upon a board that he set up with his own hand, while to the *kuan* (image-hall) he gave the name Po-yün (White Cloud).[1]

In his literary compositions the Master never began by making a rough draught ; as soon as paper lay in front of him, his brush moved rapidly and without hesitation. If some one required another copy he would re-write his theme often in a longer or shorter form than at first, and thus his works often exist in more than one form.

One night when he was talking with his disciples, he said : " About those who in ancient times acquired the Tao, the information that we can glean from books is very scanty. The lives of innumerable other Adepts went unrecorded or were recorded only in documents that are now lost. I have often mentioned to you the name of those who in recent times have obtained the Tao, all of them men with whom I have been actually

[1] The Po-yün Kuan still stands to the west of Peking, outside the walls. Its copy of the Taoist scriptures was one of the two main sources from which Père Wieger compiled his Catalogue.

acquainted. The ſtory of their lives is accurately known and their teachings are not in any way obscure. When I get the time, I intend to compose a general hiſtory of the Ch'üan Chēn seƈt, for the use of those who come after me ".

He did, indeed, before his death, give us in conversation a general idea of what he intended this work to contain. That he did not live to put these plans into execution is a faƈt that scholars of the future will certainly deplore.

APPENDIX

At the end of the *Hsi Yu Chi* are usually printed seven documents :

(1) Letter of 10th month, 1220, in which the Khan replies to Ch'ang-ch'un's letter of the 3rd month. Translated by Chavannes in *T'oung Pao*, 1908, p. 305.

(2) Edict of the Khan exempting Taoists from taxation. *T'oung Pao*, 1904, p. 370. This is dated 3rd month, 1223, and is in colloquial.

(3) Verbal instructions to A-li-hsien that Ch'ang-ch'un should be head of all monks (Taoist and Buddhist ?) in China. *T'oung Pao*, 1904, p. 372. Dated 9th month, 1223. In colloquial.

(4) Message of 11th month, 1223, sent through the Envoy Chia Ch'ang. In colloquial. " You left me and set out on your travels in the Spring and were still on the road during the great heats of the summer. I hope you suffered no inconvenience and were well supplied with post-horses. I hope that you were always provided with plenty to eat and drink and were never stinted. I hope[1] the officials at Hsüan-tē and elsewhere treated you properly. I hope that the common people came to hear you. Are you well and in good spirits ? Here I am always thinking about you, O Holy Immortal. I have never forgotten you. Do not forget me."

[1] The continual iteration of " I hope " in the English corresponds to a similar rather infantile repetition in the original.

APPENDIX

The Chinese of this message is of so elementary a nature that it is natural to wonder whether part of it at any rate was not dictated by Chingiz *in Chinese*. The usual assertion that he had no knowledge of the language is based on an anecdote that may well be apocryphal. It is likely enough that he could muster a phrase or two, such as the concluding "Wo pu . . . wang liao ni ; ni hsiu wang liao wo ".

(5) Letter from the Governor of Peking inviting Ch'ang-ch'un to live at the T'ien-ch'ang Kuan, 1223, 8th month.

(6) Letter from the Envoy Wang Tun appointing Ch'ang-ch'un Abbot of the T'ien-ch'ang Kuan. Same date as above.

(7) Letter from the Governor of Peking presenting to Ch'ang-ch'un part of the gardens of the Imperial Palace (the T'ai-chi and Ch'iung-hua).

The last three have not been translated. (5) and (6) are formal documents, of no interest. It is however interesting to read in (7), which is dated 8th month of 1226, that the reason for ceding to Ch'ang-ch'un part of the Imperial grounds was that in consequence of " recent inquisitions by contemptible people he had no longer been able to circumambulate on his Magic Staff ".[1]

From this it is obvious that the unpopularity of the Ch'üan-chēn Sect was not due only to the indiscretions of Ch'ang-ch'un's successors, but was a legacy from the Master himself.

Two more documents, not generally printed with the *Hsi Yu Chi*, belong in reality to this series :

(8) The original letter of Chingiz (composed, however, by Yeh-lü Ch'u-ts'ai) inviting Ch'ang-ch'un to visit him. The text is printed in *Chin Lien Chēng Tsung* . . .

[1] i.e., go for walks outside the monastery.

Chuan (Wieger, No. 171). The preface of this book is dated 1326. The letter (5th month, 1219) is translated by Chavannes in *T'oung Pao*, 1908, p. 399.[1] It is an elaborate literary composition containing no echo of the Khan's own voice.

(9) The Master's reply (1220, 3rd month). This was no doubt included in his later literary collection, the *Ming Tao Chi*, which was used by T'ao Tsung-i as a source for his article on Ch'ang-ch'un. The *Ming Tao Chi* no longer survives, but Ch'ang-ch'un's reply is preserved for us by T'ao Tsung-i,[2] and has been translated by Chavannes, *T'oung Pao*, 1908, p. 303.[3] It is formal and contains nothing of interest.

---

[1] See also Bretschneider, *Medieval Researches*, I, 37.
[2] In ch. X, of the *Cho Kêng Lu* (1366 A.D.).
[3] Bretschneider, *loc. cit.*, p. 40.

INDEX

11

INDEX

INDEX

INDEX

THE
BROADWAY
TRAVELLERS

Edited by Sir E. DENISON ROSS
and EILEEN POWER

"Lucky is the lover and collector of books on travel
who has the whole handsome red bound volumes of
this series on his shelves."—*Daily Telegraph.*

The Discovery and Conquest of Mexico. By *Bernal
Diaz del Castillo*, 1517-21. Translated by *Professor A. P.
Maudslay.* 15 plates and maps, 15*s.* net.

"Something more than an historical document of the first importance.
His narrative is also captivatingly readable, so that one's interest and
admiration are equally divided between the stupendous events he
records and the charming revelations he makes of his own character."
—*Saturday Review.*

Letters of Hernando Cortes, 1519-26. Translated by
J. Bayard Morris. 14 plates and maps, 15*s.* net.

"The reader has to wonder how the deeds related could possibly
have been accomplished, and marvel at the courage of such a small
band of men."—*Times Literary Supplement.*

The English American : a New Survey of the West
Indies, 1648. By *Thomas Gage.* Edited by *Professor A. P.
Newton, D.Litt.* 12 plates, 7*s.* 6*d.* net.

"His narrative is immensely interesting. Of all the excellent *Broadway
Travellers* we have not read anything better."—*Saturday Review.*

The True History of Hans Staden, 1557. Translated
by *Malcolm Letts.* Illustrated, 7*s.* 6*d.* net.

"The present translation of his adventures among the Brazilian
cannibals now make Staden's story available to a larger public, and
the story warrants it, not only because of its sensatioual qualities. '
—*New Statesman.*

Travels in Persia, 1627-9. By *Thomas Herbert*. Edited by *Sir William Foster*, C.I.E. 13 plates, 7*s*. 6*d*. net.

"One of the best of seventeenth century travel narratives."—*Times*.
"This delightful classic."—*Saturday Review*.

Travels of Ibn Battuta, 1324-54. Translated by *H. A. R. Gibb*. 8 plates, 7*s*. 6*d*. net.

"One of the most fascinating travel-books of all time."—*Times Literary Supplement*. "The entire book, beautifully translated, has intense interest. The account of the court of the Sultan at Delhi is as exciting as anything of the kind I ever read."—ARNOLD BENNETT, in *Evening Standard*.

Memorable Description of the East-Indian Voyage, 1618-25. By *Willem Ysbrantsz Bontekoe*. Translated by *Mrs. C. B. Bodde-Hodgkinson* and *Professor Pieter Geyl, Lit.D.* 10 plates, 7*s*. 6*d*. net.

"Fire and shipwreck, fights ashore and afloat, the pitting of ceaseless patience and resource against fate, these things make one understand why this book, famous in its original tongue, has but to be savoured in translation to gain an equal popularity."—*Manchester Guardian*.

Travels into Spain. By *Madame d'Aulnoy*, 1691. Edited by *R. Foulché-Delbosc*. 4 plates, 7*s*. 6*d*. net.

"Of all literary fakes this is surely the most impudent, ingenious and successful. Despite its factual falseness, it is intellectually and emotionally the real thing."—*Saturday Review*.

Travels and Adventures of Pero Tafur. (1435-1439). Translated by *Malcolm Letts*. 8 plates, 7*s*. 6*d*. net.

"A document of unique interest, it is a picture of Europe at the most critical moment of its history."—SIR EDMUND GOSSE, in *Sunday Times*.

Akbar and the Jesuits. Translated from the "Histoire" of *Father Pierre du Jarric, S.J.*, by *C. H. Payne*. 8 plates, 7*s*. 6*d*. net.

"A serious and intensely interesting piece of work."—*Guardian*.

Don Juan of Persia, a Shi'ah Catholic, (1560-1604). Translated by *Guy le Strange*. 3 Maps, 7*s*. 6*d*. net.

"The record of an intrepid Persian nobleman who undertook a special diplomatic mission to various Courts of Europe in the interests of his King. A fine story of gallant adventure."—*New Statesman*.

The Diary of Henry Teonge, Chaplain on board H.M.'s Ships *Assistance, Bristol,* and *Royal Oak* (1675-1679). Edited by *G. E. Manwaring.* 8 plates, 7*s.* 6*d.* net.

"This diary is history ; and more can be learnt from it of actual life under Charles II than from many able academic books."—*Observer.*

Memoirs of an Eighteenth-Century Footman : the Life and Travels of John Macdonald (1745-1779). Edited by *John Beresford.* 8 plates, 7*s.* 6*d.* net.

"Exceedingly entertaining travels, instinct with life."—*Times Literary Supplement.* "Simply packed with interest."—*Sunday Times.*

Nova Francia : a Description of Acadia, 1606. By *Marc Lescarbot.* Edited by *H. P. Biggar.* 2 maps, 7*s.* 6*d.* net.

"The early beginnings of the French settlement of Acadia are delightfully narrated. The book is full of gaiety and sound information."—*Spectator.*

Travels in Tartary, Thibet, and China, (1844-6). By *E. R. Huc* and *M. Gabet.* Introduction by *Professor Paul Pelliot.* With a map. 2 vols, 15*s.* net.

"One of the most alluring travel books ever written. To read it is like seeing the scenes described. The edition is admirable."—ARNOLD BENNETT in *Evening Standard.*

Clavijo's Embassy to Tamerlane, (1403-6). Translated by *Guy le Strange.* 7 maps and plans, 7*s.* 6*d.* net.

"So keen and intelligent an observer and so lively a retailer of travel gossip that a popular edition of his work has long been overdue. . . . this remarkable book."—*New Statesman.*

Commentaries of Captain Ruy Freyre de Andrada, 1647. Edited by *C. R. Boxer.* 8 plates and maps, 7*s.* 6*d.* net.

"The main interest of this most vivacious chronicle lies in the account it gives of the siege and capture of the island-fortress of Ormuz, which was the Portuguese Gibraltar."—*Spectator.*

Jahangir and the Jesuits. By *Fernao Guerreiro, S. J.* Translated by *C. H. Payne, M.A.* 4 plates, 7*s.* 6*d.* net.

"Full of splendour and strange scenes."—*New Statesman.*

Jewish Travellers, from the Ninth to the Eighteenth Century. Translated by *Elkan Adler.* 8 plates and map, 7*s.* 6*d.* net.

"Narratives full of interesting and curious information presented in a readable and scholarly version."—*Manchester Guardiain.*

The Travels of Marco Polo. Translated from the text of *L. F. Benedetto* by *Professor Aldo Ricci*. 11 plates and maps, 7s. 6d. net.

"For most readers the *Broadway Travellers* edition of this most famous of travel books will supersede all others in English." — *Discovery*.

Travels in India By *Captain Basil Hall, R.N., F.R.S.* Edited by *Professor H. G. Rawlinson*. 4 plates, 7s. 6d. net.

"Contains very interesting pictures of life in India during the latter days of 'The Company' and some remarkable scenes of extraordinary interest. His vivid narrative offers his reader only too much to think about." — *Spectator*.

The Travels of an Alchemist. Translated by *Arthur Waley*. With a map, 7s. 6d. net.

"An account of the journey of Ch'ang-Ch'un from China to the Hindukush in the early thirteenth century. A highly fascinating book, written as brightly as the best modern journalism." — *Everyman*.

The First Englishmen in India. Edited by *J. Courtenay Locke*. 4 plates, 7s. 6d. net.

"Here are the narratives of the sturdy Elizabethan merchants who travelled to India and whose reports of their experiences led to the founding of the East India Company." — *Spectator*.

An Account of Tibet : the Travels of *Ippolito Desideri*, of Pistoia, S. J., 1712-27. Edited by *Filippo De Filippi*. 16 plates, 7s. 6d. net. net.

"The present publication, in English, is the first edition of the whole work. It will be a classic of travel and a monument of heroic devotion. Desideri was intelligent, observant, humorous, sympathetic, and Franciscan in his charity and faith. He was interested in everything he saw. Many of his descriptions of the country might have come out of a modern book. The *Broadway Travellers* is a fine series, but no volume yet published in it exceeds this in interest or is fuller of surprises." — *Sunday Times*.

Sir Anthony Sherley and his Persian Adventure. By *Sir E. Denison Ross*. 10 plates and maps, 8vo, 7s. 6d. net.

"Rich in material that is interesting to the historian and to the student of the customs, religion, and culture of the times." — *Scotsman*.

Published by
GEORGE ROUTLEDGE & SONS, LTD.
Broadway House, Carter Lane, London, E.C.4

9 781406 797145